78

How Christians Can Save America

Peter Heck

Library of Congress Cataloging-in-Publication Data

ISBN-13: 978-1461186274
ISBN-10: 1461186277

Published in the United States by
Attaboy Press

a division of Attaboy Productions, Inc.
2004 Waverly Drive
Kokomo, IN 46902

For more information on Attaboy Productions, Inc., please visit:
www.peterheck.com

Distributed in cooperation with
CreateSpace
7290 B. Investment Drive
Charleston, SC 29418

To Mom and Dad, for putting my feet upon the straight and narrow path...

Dr. Martin, for teaching me how best to walk it...

J, for giving me reason to every day.

CONTENTS

PART ONE: THE REALIZATION

PART TWO: THE REFORMATION

PART THREE: THE REVOLUTION

PART FOUR: THE RENEWAL

PART FIVE: THE REBIRTH

Part One
The Realization

He who is void of virtuous attachment in private life is, or very soon will be, void of all regard for his country.

— Samuel Adams

CHAPTER ONE

A New Doctor

Imagine going to the doctor with a runny nose. After a full examination, your doctor excuses himself from the room only to return moments later with a brand new box of Kleenex. He hands it to you and advises you to use the tissues as needed for your condition. Confused, you pay your bill and leave, Kleenex in hand.

A week later, you return to your doctor still hampered by the same runny nose, but this time with the addition of a sore throat. Your doctor patiently reexamines you and again excuses himself before returning with yet another box of Kleenex...and a package of Halls cough drops for your throat. Even more bewildered this time, you dutifully pay the receptionist the price of your second office visit and are on your way.

But in just a matter of days, you make a third trip back to the exam room, not only with a runny nose and sore throat, but now also a burning fever. After yet another thorough examination, your doctor appears puzzled. But nevertheless he leaves briefly, returning with a third box of Kleenex, another package of Halls cough drops…and now an ice pack for your fever.

It is difficult to think that anyone would continue seeking the services of such an obviously incompetent physician. It's equally difficult to believe that such a doctor would be able to find patients willing to continue financing his practice if this was the extent of his medical expertise.

Once word got out that this doctor was capable of treating only the symptoms of an illness, rather than eliminating its root cause, the demand for his services would dwindle to extinction quite rapidly.

Yet, this is exactly the scenario that American society has been facing for the last several decades. Confronting a growing list of cultural problems, we have been consistently reassured by leaders of both political parties that they have just what we need. However, despite faithfully paying our ever increasing bill for their services, we find that their diagnosis is lacking. We find ourselves back in the exam room still searching for a cure to our original problem while experiencing newer and uglier symptoms, all while these professionals look for more Kleenex.

Maybe it's time for a patient revolt?

In doing preparation for one of my radio programs, I was sifting through some polling data conducted by the well respected Pew Research Center. In their most recent survey on the American religious landscape, they reported that 78.4% of U.S. citizens claimed Christian affiliation.[1]

To be sure, there is a great deal of denominational difference in that number. It includes Protestants and Catholics, as well as Mormon, Jehovah's Witnesses, and Orthodox churches. There are liberal sects and conservative ones, fundamentalist and extra-biblical adherents. Still, 78% of Americans claim allegiance to the Christian tradition.

Attempting to reconcile that number with the condition of American culture is mind-boggling.

To say that our society has reached a crisis point is so patently obvious that it insults the intellect to even pretend otherwise.

Across the country, the eleven o'clock news has become little more than a nightly recitation of all the tragedies occurring that day: from rapes to murders to molestations and assaults...the news itself should carry with it a "mature audiences only" rating.

And while some quibble over the exact rankings, there is no questioning the fact that in categories like violent crime, illegal drug use, greed, child abuse, divorce, teen pregnancies, and voluntary abortions, the United States is among the world's worst.

But even more concerning – if that's possible – is the fact that our cultural leaders are either oblivious to, or unwilling to confront, the root causes of our dilemma. They take great pride in championing plans and programs that at best sweep out the cobwebs, while doing absolutely nothing about the spider. Then, when the cobwebs return the next day in even greater number, rather than being shamed by their failure to solve the problem, they use it as justification to grant them even more power, hijack even more resources, and confiscate even more money to waste on their Kleenex, cough drops, and ice packs.

So while the other 22% may certainly read and digest what follows, this book is written to the 78%.

It's written to serve as a motivation for the three-fourths of Americans who possess the answer to our problems, and the cure to our disease. May the following pages serve as a catalyst for us, the 78, to find the courage to declare the obvious...

America, it's time for a new doctor.

CHAPTER TWO

It's Up To Us

Several years ago in the early days of my teaching career, I decided to put myself through graduate school. Quickly realizing the financial burden that placed on an already thin budget, I took a summer job as a janitor/groundskeeper to help supplement my payments.

Though I would regard my boss those summers, a man named Greg Dryer, as the best among the many great bosses I have worked for in my life, I think it's safe to say I wasn't his most spectacular employee. In fact, I became infamous for destroying more equipment than anyone in the history of that high school's maintenance department.

And with every new accident – splitting blades by mowing over stumps to shattering windshields to inadvertently spilling permanent traffic paint all over the freshly paved parking lot – Mr. Dryer's reaction was always the same. He would walk up to the scene of the incident, tip his cowboy hat up a little higher on his brow, sigh and say, "And you've got a Masters Degree? Pete, you prove to me over and over again that educated don't mean smart."

Truer words have never been spoken.

It is astonishing how many bright and educated people totally fail to grasp the link between the crises we face as a culture, and the breakdown of morality we have been experiencing for decades.

We're repeatedly told our problems are economic. Even supposedly staunch conservative Governors like Mitch Daniels of Indiana and Chris Christie of New Jersey beg us to ignore "social issues," and first put our financial house in order. Specifically, Daniels called for, "a truce on the so-called social issues," saying that until we resolve our budget and monetary problems, "We're going to just have to agree to get along for a little while" on matters of morality.[1]

But common sense guides us otherwise. What causes debt if it is not irresponsibility and a lack of stewardship by those entrusted with public monies? What causes exploitation in the market if it is not self-indulgence and greed? In other words, those who are truly interested in solving our slide into economic oblivion are those who are willing not to call a truce with immorality, but rather expose and confront it.

The same can be said for every domestic or cultural problem we face.

Take violent crime. For years we have suffered the idiocy that says increasing the amount of gun laws – adding waiting periods, mandatory registration, licensing brackets, and assault weapons bans – will alleviate our growing crisis of gun-related offenses. It's difficult to know whether those arguing this way honestly believe what they're saying, given the absurdity of such a position.

It is fine to debate the merits of those laws, and we may find some to be logical and appropriate. But pretending that they will have any significant impact on slowing America's problem with violent crime is beyond silly. Obviously those perpetrating hostile offenses are not deterred by laws in the first place. Therefore, additional statutes will be useless in solving a dilemma that, at its core, is driven by passions unbridled by a strong moral center.

Our abject poverty of such common sense is seen also in the debate over teenage pregnancy. I will never forget a conversation I had with Jesse, a caller to my radio program, on the issue of condom distribution in public high schools:

Jesse: The thing is that kids are going to have sex whether we want them to or not. So at least if they are, they should be given condoms to protect them. Otherwise they're going to end up pregnant or with diseases or something else. I don't understand how anybody can be wanting kids to get diseases.

Peter: Jesse, do you really think I or anyone else like me honestly wants kids to get diseases?

Jesse: Well I don't know, you must if you want them to have sex without a condom.

Peter: Jesse, what I'm advocating is the teaching of personal responsibility. I'm talking about making kids aware of the only way to avoid those difficult and dangerous circumstances you mentioned. I'm –

Jesse: Yeah, and I'm talking about saving kids lives. You know, you're against abortion, right?

Peter: Yes Jesse, I'm against abortion.

Jesse: Then I can't understand why you are not wanting condoms handed out. Because without them, more people get pregnant, and then have abortions. It's just –

Peter: Hold on, hold on, hold on, Jesse. You can't make a leap of logic like that, first of all. It's a logical fallacy, what you just did. But more importantly than that, let me ask you a question…a serious question…when you hand out condoms in schools – in health class or whatever – what are you encouraging?

Jesse: What are you encouraging?

Peter: Yes, when you hand out condoms to kids, what are you encouraging them to do?

Jesse: You're encouraging them to have safe
          sex.

Peter: Okay, you're close. I don't need you
          to describe what kind of activity
          you're encouraging, just tell me the
          activity. What are you encouraging?

Jesse: Yeah, you're encouraging them to
          have safe sex. Rather than –

Peter: Whoa wait a minute, we can have the
          debate over whether condoms are
          "safe" or not in a minute. I just want
          to know what you're encouraging.

Jesse: Safe sex.

Peter: No, Jesse, you're not being honest. I
          will let you stay on the line and we
          can talk at length about the success
          rate of condoms and how safe they
          really are in preventing diseases, how
          often they rupture, the frequency of
          pregnancy coming even with condom
          use – we'll talk about all of that in a
          bit. But right now, I just want to know
          what behavior you're encouraging
          when you hand out condoms to kids.
          Don't describe the behavior by saying
          safe or unsafe. Just tell me the
          behavior itself. What are you
          encouraging?

Jesse: I'm not going to say what you want
          me to say.[2]

Jesse never did say it. But he didn't have to. It is an affront to common sense when you attempt to solve problems that come solely from premarital sex between teenagers by encouraging premarital sex between teenagers. The truth is that I think Jesse really did have the best interest of kids at heart. But despite the best of intentions, he was advocating the purchase of Kleenex boxes to solve the runny nose of teen pregnancy.

Jesse is far from alone. Our society has become so overrun with nonsense advocated by self-proclaimed experts on various social problems, that many of us – the 78 – have succumbed to their way of thinking.

How else can you explain the travesty that has occurred within the pro-life movement in America? Far from staunchly advocating and defending an unalienable right to life, the pro-life movement has compromised their position by willfully negotiating with evil. The strategy has become to pass ultrasound laws, parental consent laws, and waiting periods before abortion can take place.

But what do these laws, when enacted, actually accomplish? They codify a legal declaration that after showing a woman a fuzzy picture, getting a parent's signature on a paper, or waiting 24 hours, it is then acceptable to kill a human child in the womb. And this is done with the blessing of the pro-life movement?!

How devastating that we have now arrived at a point where those supposedly advocating a right to life have willingly conceded their morally superior position by writing laws that theoretically state, "Do this first...and then you can kill the baby?"

Is it any wonder that after 38 years of such a strategy, over one million American children continue to be sacrificed annually to the false god of convenience?

Such an approach is not morally grounded, but rather built upon a humanistic utilitarian philosophy that actually undermines the entire cause of life. How can you claim to believe that life is sacred while simultaneously authoring the very legislation that provides an acceptable method to destroy it? It is the moral equivalent to negotiating with terrorists that if they will release one hostage, they have your permission to kill the remaining 99.

But sadly, this is the kind of thought you would expect from a society whose moral fiber has torn free from its moorings, and is left flapping in the breeze of relativism, rendering the masses totally incapable of grounded, rational thought.

It's the kind of thought that convinces us that more after school specials on ABC will help the underage drinking crisis, or that self-esteem class will alleviate the tragedy of suicide.

Yet as we continue treating our symptoms, the illness grows larger and stronger until it eventually manifests itself in unimaginable ways.

I was nearing the end of my sophomore year in college on April 20, 1999. As I walked past the dorm lounge, I noticed a large number of guys standing there in silence, watching the big screen TV. I walked in to see images of young people running across a school campus with their hands on their heads as though they were in a military camp. SWAT teams dressed all in black, police crime scene tape, teenagers being loaded onto stretchers – as the tragedy of the Columbine massacre unfolded before my eyes, it all seemed surreal.

I remember being pretty fixated on the aftermath of the slaughter, watching multiple interviews with victims, witnesses, parents and friends of those involved. But nothing stood out to me more in those days than the analysis and explanations provided by the media and their so-called experts. These were the people that we were trusting to tell us why two high school aged kids would ever perpetrate such a violent act. We were turning to them to explain what could cause behavior like this.

And there, sitting behind their half-glasses with mountains of sociological survey data, and speaking to media elites like Katie Couric, they espoused the commonly accepted culprits: Eric Harris and Dylan Klebold were prompted by violent video games and movies. They were ostracized at school without many friends. They suffered from Attention Deficit Disorder and other medical conditions. And that was it. Those were the answers we were supposed to accept. And amazingly, such sophistry, such unimaginative and painfully inadequate conclusions received the stamp of approval from our culture.

Even then Vice President Al Gore, in his eloquent memorial address to the slain, seemed to concur with these non-answers as he stated, "If you are a parent, your children need your attention…We must have the courage not to look away from those who feel despised and rejected…Children look to us…We must protect them from the violence and cruelty in our popular culture…It is too easy for a young child to get a gun…We need to look for the earliest signs of trouble -- and teach our children to resolve their differences with reason and conscience, not with flashes of passion."[3]

Perhaps it was at that moment, listening to the Vice President, when the devastating reality dawned on me that our society either doesn't want to understand, or it lacks the courage to admit the truth. Don't get me wrong, I agree with most everything that Vice President Gore said, and it's important to understand how those concerns he articulated can fuel aggression in those who are already off the tracks. But our only hope of preventing future tragedies like Columbine comes from curing the disease that has derailed young people like Harris and Klebold – not from eliminating peripheral toxins that merely accelerate the evil that is already festering.

Let me make it personal. Obviously, I'm not bragging about what follows, but rather simply making a point. When I was in high school and college, my friends and I loved to play violent video games like *James Bond GoldenEye: 007.* Rumor is that some of them (not me, of course) even skipped classes on occasion to have an all-day Bond fest. We watched violent movies as well. And not the violent movies with redeeming qualities like *Saving Private Ryan*, *We Were Soldiers*, or *The Patriot.* No, we're talking Hollywood slasher movies like the *Scream* franchise. Consider also that with a Dad in the U.S. Air Force, my family moved frequently. Having friends wasn't always a luxury for me – so much so that I invented them (Clarice the Mule, based off the movie *The Apple Dumpling Gang Rides Again*, was my imaginary friend until I was in the 5th grade). And when it comes to Attention Deficit Disorder, the only reason I wasn't diagnosed with it as a child was because it wasn't in existence then.

Why do I mention all this? Because despite possessing each of these "causes of Columbine," and despite the ease with which I could have gotten my hands on guns and weapons, I never once even thought about killing myself or my classmates. Does that reality mean that those movies and video games are edifying and appropriate? Of course not. But what it means is that they fall woefully short in explaining the root cause of the Columbine massacre.

In his memorial speech, Gore challenged, "In a culture rife with violence – where too many young people place too little value on a human life – we can rise up and say no more."[4] Indeed we can, if we are willing. Are we?

Will Al Gore give a speech, or will Katie Couric run a news special of this nature? Are they ready to address the root cause, the disease, the spider that is infecting our society? Are they prepared to be serious about getting to the heart of our cultural problems? Are they willing to follow the evidence where it leads?

Unfortunately, all signs indicate the contrary. They are content to accept benign explanations that only begin to scratch at the surface of the dilemmas we face, so long as those explanations are offered by someone with a degree from an approved institution and are bathed in the shallow rhetoric of tolerance. Any appeal to moral authority, personal responsibility, and eternal expectation is to be expelled from our airwaves, our courtrooms, and lecture halls. And thus, the fairly self-evident understanding of Columbine evades the conscience of our people.

After all, only a culture starved of truth fails to grasp that the tragedies unfolding daily in our schools, our homes, and on our streets are the direct result of an intentional deprivation of moral grounding. When you teach young people from their first day in public high school biology class that human life is nothing but a cosmic accident with no ultimate value, destiny, or purpose...when you teach young people that their existence is nothing but the worthless conglomeration of molecules that came together purely by chance billions of years ago...when you teach young people that murdering an infant is a choice...when you teach young people that killing off the unwanted elderly is humane...when you teach young people that suicide is acceptable if it's assisted by a physician...when you teach young people that eliminating the sick and the terminal is ethical and justifiable...when you teach them such things, you have successfully ingrained into the minds of an entire generation that life itself is worthless.

How then can it be surprising when those same young people treat life as though it is worthless? In short, if you intentionally build your castle on the beach, don't be surprised when the sand shifts from under it, causing it to collapse.

If Mr. Gore truly wanted to know why "too many young people place too little value on a human life," he would be speaking to those very realities. If Katie Couric wanted to know what drives young people to act in such evil ways, she would discard the video game talk and start addressing why Eric Harris wrote in his journal before the Columbine murders,

"NATURAL SELECTION. F---ers should be shot."[5]
She would note the significance of why he wore a t-shirt the day of the slaughter with the words "Natural Selection" printed in bold.[6] If our cultural elites truly wanted an answer as to why kids don't act "right," they would be dealing with the plague of moral relativism in our culture. After all, why should kids act right when we teach them every day that there is no "right?"

But these are the questions that cannot be asked. These are the answers that are not given.

Here is the painful truth we must acknowledge: our cultural, political, educational and media leaders are not interested in addressing the fundamental questions because they don't agree with the fundamental solutions. They are like those described by the prophet Ezekiel when he wrote, "They have eyes to see but do not see and ears to hear but do not hear, for they are a rebellious people."[7]

Which means, quite simply, it's up to us.

Part Two
The Reformation

We are in hard times. The church is barely surviving. We are to be the awakened. We are to be the ones — the church of the living God — saying, 'That is enough, and I will not tolerate it any longer.'

— Charles R. Swindoll

CHAPTER THREE

THE CONSCIENCE OF AMERICA

The ability of the 78 to provide any path to cultural deliverance rests entirely on our ability of self-diagnosis. Blaming the 22 for our plight is dishonest and delusional. To put it bluntly, the church is failing America.

This devastating reality became self-evident to me when I received the following correspondence from the ministerial staff of a local church that had contacted me about speaking to their congregation:

Peter,

First and foremost, as the leadership of the church we want to let you know how much we appreciate your ministry and your stand for morality in our community. Your convictions are inspiring and the fearlessness with which you defend Biblical principles is reassuring to all of us.

As you know, we expressed interest in bringing you in to present one of your four-part series on Christians and the culture. We thank you for the information and sample DVDs you sent us for your *America's Foundation of Faith*, *Pillars of the Faith*, and *A Christian Response to the Unmentionables* series.

In discussing this with the church board, we have decided that given your controversial position as a radio host and political columnist, having you in for an officially sanctioned church event could give the illusion that the church was putting its stamp of approval on your political views.

As we're sure you understand, that could cause us some potential problems regarding our tax-exempt status with the IRS. Further, a few of our board members are aware of parishioners who would vehemently object to your messages on abortion and homosexuality specifically, and if we brought you in, might (God forbid) leave our church.

While we regard your message as one of Biblical truth, as ministers and leaders of our local congregation we must be looking out for the well being of the body as a whole. For those reasons alone, we feel we must decline our original proposal to have you come and speak to us at this time.

Thank you for your understanding, and keep fighting the good fight.

I was, and remain, at a loss to know how to respond to that message. My astonishment has nothing to do with their ultimate decision to un-invite me – the choice to bring in a guest speaker is obviously at the total discretion of those leading their congregation.

But I honestly find myself hoping that their stated rationale was an attempt to find a polite way of letting me down easy, rather than an accurate representation of their feelings. I hope that perhaps my speaking fee was too high for them, or that maybe they were unimpressed with samples of my work and just didn't know how to tell me that directly.

I know it seems odd that I am hoping a group of ministers were untruthful with me. But in this case, I am overly convinced that dishonesty is preferable to the alternative. Because if these words do convey their true position, consider the bizarre contradictions and frightening conclusions they come to.

After applauding my "fearlessness" in defending truth in the first paragraph, the remainder of the letter is an attempt to excuse their own cowardice. The ministers apparently believe that the content of my message is Biblically sound. And yet because the proclamation of that Biblically grounded message might potentially offend members in their congregation who do not wish to be made uncomfortable, this ministerial staff thinks it best to avoid such controversy.

I have heard of ministers protecting their flock, but this is the first time I've ever encountered ones who seek to protect them from being exposed to (what the ministers themselves acknowledge to be) Biblical morality.

It begs the question as to what is motivating the ministers' unease over losing members of their congregation. Is it driven by concern for their souls? Perhaps. But the exclusive nature of the Gospel message – that Jesus Christ alone is the way to the Father – smacks of the very type of controversial sermonizing that they seem to discourage and frown upon.

The more likely explanation is that a loss of members means a loss of tithes and offerings. This conclusion may be somewhat speculative, but it is corroborated by the ministers' phony IRS excuse.

Though secular humanists have attempted to bully the church into silence on matters relating to politics and society with threats to undo their tax-exempt status, they don't have a leg to stand on. As Erik Stanley, senior legal counsel of the Alliance Defense Fund explains:

> Arguing that a tax agency should hold veto power over sermon content is like arguing that the Department of Transportation should decide a school lunch menu. Pastors spoke freely about the policy positions of candidates for elective office throughout American history, even endorsing or opposing candidates from the pulpit, without anyone ever questioning whether churches should remain tax exempt. It was common, indeed expected, for pastors to speak in support of or in opposition to candidates until the Johnson

Amendment was inserted quietly into the tax code in 1954, with no legislative analysis or debate.

Most scholars recognize that the amendment had nothing to do with churches. It was cleverly designed to silence some nonprofit organizations who opposed Lyndon B. Johnson's Senate campaign in Texas. But that hasn't stopped activist groups from wielding the IRS weapon to silence churches across the country. The tax agency's rule is unconstitutional because it muzzles free speech and improperly entangles the state in church affairs.

The state cannot demand the surrender of constitutional rights for a church to remain tax exempt.[1]

Ministers who allow themselves to be intimidated by these unconstitutional threats should note that in recent election cycles, preachers from around the country have participated in something called the "Pulpit Initiative." This was a coordinated event where ministers evaluated candidates for elective office based on how their views matched up with Scripture.

I hosted one of the participating ministers on my radio program. Dr. Ron Johnson, Jr. told me that he and several other participants went so far as to send letters to the IRS informing them of their plans to make formal endorsements of candidates from their pulpits.[2] The IRS did not pursue a single case.

The tax-exempt warning is nothing but pure bluster from those who would castrate the church and render it impotent in addressing cultural and societal issues from a Biblical perspective. That so many ministers of the Gospel willingly submit to such a phony threat is alarming.

Moreover, suppose the threat wasn't phony. Suppose the authorities and principalities of man stood ready to punish ministers who dared to expound upon Biblical truth in the public square. Could the current leadership of the American church be counted on to boldly and courageously be obedient to God at any cost?

The correspondence I received from the ministerial staff concerned about my offensively Biblical message seems to provide the disquieting answer.

Yes, it is only one letter. Yes, it is but one piece of anecdotal evidence. But I think it is representative of what is occurring with frightening regularity in our nation's churches, which then poses some serious questions for us to address.

If the objection of certain parishioners to the Biblical content of a sermon is enough to discourage the staff from sharing such a message, what role does that church then play?

If, "the love of money is a root of all kinds of evil,"[3] then how dangerous is it that offerings and budgets have become the primary concern in the institution that exists to confront evil?

If ministers are paralyzed with fear over the thought of alienating someone in their congregation by preaching truth, have they not surrendered their ability to exhort righteousness and condemn wickedness?

If concern over offending the masses supersedes the church's mission to correct and rebuke misguided beliefs and thoughts, has that church not neutered itself to the point of being a mere social club?

Sadly, those words best describe some of this country's largest congregations. The tragic dilemma found in our pulpits is simply this: far from being the object, proclamation of truth has come to be regarded as an obstacle for those guiding the church in America.

Truth divides. It pits right against wrong, good against bad, yes against no, and true against false.

And as people, guided by a fallen human nature, inevitably cross that line with regularity, it is the seemingly unpleasant responsibility of the church to illuminate the truth that distinguishes between the two sides. Needless to say, few react warmly to having transgressions they are freely participating in condemned as improper.

Their resentment is complicated further by a culture that is increasingly moving to adopt a post-modern philosophy of moral relativism. Self-evident truth has been replaced by self-determined truth. An entire generation has now been trained from its earliest days to believe that no one set of ideas is better than another, and that tolerance means approval.

Consequently, while the truth may indeed liberate our souls, it also provokes earthly discord. The Author and personification of truth Himself told us to expect as much when He said, "Do you think I came to bring peace on earth? No, I tell you, but division. From now on there will be five in one family divided against each other, three against two and two against three.

They will be divided, father against son and son against father, mother against daughter and daughter against mother."[4]

Jesus didn't desire division. Still, He was explaining to us that there will always be those whose pride causes them to reject and live in rebellion to the truth. But rather than accept the words of the Savior as accurate and work diligently to find ways to bring people into obedience, the American church is taking the backwards approach of silencing the proclamation of truth in the hopes of eliminating all division.

This futile attempt to prove that we know better than Jesus demands the avoidance of controversy in order to swell the ranks. Success becomes measured not by hearts changed and minds transformed, but rather seats filled.

Churches no longer seem to be competing with the forces of darkness for the souls of man, but rather competing with each other to see who can have the biggest building, largest budget, and highest attendance. And since standing firm on Biblical principles typically gets in the way of such ends, many of our churches decide it's best to just forgo anything perceived as divisive, and adopt a "whatever" mentality that accommodates the doctrinal preferences of virtually everyone simply by pretending that the differences are inconsequential.

What has resulted from that new philosophy is the emergence of a watered down Christianity. Perhaps "lukewarm" is the better term for it.

Sunday School is replaced with coffee and donuts. Memory verses are replaced by arts and crafts. Bible trivia is replaced by game nights. Communion tables are removed for aesthetic purposes. And in what is surely the most devastating example of this perilous state of affairs, crosses are removed from church grounds to avoid "intimidating" the outsider.

Stephen Lawson's chilling observation is true: "In a strange twist, the preaching of the cross is now foolishness, not only to the world, but also to the contemporary church."[5]

The nation's most prominent ministers are those who purposefully steer clear of anything that might remotely be regarded as judgmental, instead designing sermons that are more appropriately described as "self-help" seminars. For the sake of bringing in great numbers, they offer doctrinally generic – though positive and uplifting – sermonettes that are often times void of any Scripture whatsoever.

Then, in a deadly combination of pride and moral confusion, they justify their milquetoast brand of Christianity by pointing to their sold-out stadiums and touting that non-Christians and atheists are among their most loyal congregants.[6]

Obviously I'm not implying that a non-believer should be intentionally made to feel unwelcome in the House of God. But as a minister of the Gospel message, if the atheist feels comfortable and the Muslim feels at peace with your sermon, there's something dreadfully wrong with your commitment to the primary mission of urgently seeking and saving the lost.

Beloved Bible teacher Charles R. Swindoll – a man for whom I hold the utmost respect and admiration – powerfully rebuked this ignorant mindset:

Pastors who are committed to Biblical
exposition must have a confrontive element
in their preaching. It is better to be divided
by truth than be united in error. It is better to
speak the truth that hurts and heals than
falsehood that comforts and kills. It's not
love, it's not friendship if we fail to declare
the whole counsel of God. It is better to be
hated for telling the truth than to be loved for
telling a lie. It is better to stand alone with
the truth than to stand for wrong with a
multitude.[7]

In other words, the country church minister who
preaches truth to a congregation of 50 is having a far
greater impact for the Kingdom of God than a mega-
minister who avoids truth so that he can fill 50,000 seats
every Sunday.

Of course, Swindoll's admonition makes sense
only if you believe that the church's priority is to point
all people to Christ as Lord, press them towards Godly
living, and warn them of the consequences of sin. The
modern American church, however, seems to have
different objectives.

After all, saving souls and impacting the culture
for Christ can hinder budgets, hamper building
projects, and stunt the growth of the next mega-
ministry.

I should disclose that I am not a minister, and
therefore I harbor no jealousy for those with massive
congregations. In fact, far from there being anything
wrong with a mega-church, Christians are commanded
to make disciples of all people. My concern is that the

church in America has grown proficient at making congregants, not disciples.

This has profound long-term ramifications. While true disciples are passionate about their beliefs, mere congregants often times struggle to even identify what their beliefs are. The same Pew study that found 78% of Americans claiming the Christian tradition, also revealed that atheists and agnostics scored better than Christians when it came to basic religious knowledge.[8]

While embarrassing, we can hardly be surprised at such a result. The strategy of watering down the faith for the sake of filling the offering plates has been, and continues to be, a colossal mistake that threatens the existence of the church in America. What good are the ranks, after all, if they are not properly trained?

Many churchgoers today are wrongly told that the Bible is the weapon of choice for Christians in confronting the world. But the Bible is merely a compilation of books...an armory, if you will. The power – the weapon – is in the Word.

Consider an army that goes out to do battle with no bullets in their guns. They wouldn't last very long in the field. And yet, this is the very mentality that is permeating the American church. We tell Christians who are leery about sharing their faith, "Oh, just go talk to unbelievers, God will tell you what to say." Every time I hear this nonsense I want to scream. We concoct this fantasy scenario where God is going to appear before us in a difficult conversation with atheists and reveal some great morsel of truth just in the nick of time to allow us to win the argument. How absurd.

God isn't going to tell us the answer...because

He's already told us! His revelation of truth is within our grasp. If we choose not to open it, not to study it, and not to learn it, that's not God's fault...it's ours.

I remember a heartbreaking conversation I had just a few years ago with a former student from early on in my teaching career. For the most part, he had been raised in the church since he was in elementary school, and when I had him in class, he had even talked about going into the youth ministry. I lost touch with him after he graduated until we ran into one another several years later. Far from entering the ministry, this young man had become a committed Darwinist, totally rejecting any belief in the existence of God. I offered to sit and talk with him about his questions sometime, but he politely declined. He had been raised in the church, he reasoned, and what he heard there just wasn't nearly as logical or compelling as what he heard from his university professors.

What happened? He had been enticed by the false promise of no accountability that comes from shunning a moral authority. Another way of putting it: he went to do battle against the world with no bullets in his gun. How many other young people is the church failing in this same way?

Coming to services on Sunday morning and seeing a few verses flash up on the projection screen, combined with having a family Bible with your name engraved on the front does not count for the kind of training necessary to do battle with the proud notions that set themselves up against the knowledge of God.[9] Always being prepared to give an answer to anyone who asks you to give a reason for the hope that you have,[10] as the Apostle Peter instructs, means that believers should be diligently and faithfully studying the Word on a daily basis. And churches should be training them how to do that.

But instead we're focused on other things, as our church leaders have allowed stadium seating, theater quality surround sound and digital plasma screens the size of city buses to sadly taken precedence. There is nothing wrong with technological gadgetry and audiovisual aesthetics. Indeed, they can provide a powerful way to transmit a message of truth.

But rather than be used in such a way, the focus placed upon these elements often becomes a mere marketing strategy to improve the curb appeal of the church. Modern ministry experts now agree that if we make our Sunday services more like a convention, concert, or coffeehouse, we will attract more visitors. An inordinate amount of church planning books have been written that describe in detail the way to effectively grow your congregation in the information age: hipper music, smart lighting, theater reclining seats, concessions and couches.

I will never forget a conversation I had with a man who was espousing this very mindset as he attempted to sell me a book he had just written on how to "modernize the church." He said to me, "You know, if the church in America would just model itself off this book, great things would happen."

I really wasn't trying to offend him when I sighed heavily, picked up a copy of the Bible and said, "Actually, I think we just need to once again start taking seriously the book we've already got." Great things would happen if we did.

But we aren't moving in that direction. The church's mission has become entertaining a crowd rather than educating a congregation. And consequently, as counterintuitive as this may sound, the church has become an impediment to the cause of Christ in our country.

The deterioration of American culture is not surprising given what has happened in the American church.

For generations, this institution has served as the moral conscience of our nation. From the days of Jonathan Edwards, the American pulpit has provided clarity in the midst of social confusion, offered strength in the depths of national despair, and aided our people in navigating through the minefields of some remarkably complex ethical challenges and moral dilemmas.

Historically, it has been the energetic church that has seasoned the landscape of our political and social discourse with the salt of truth, and boldly shone the light necessary to expose shortcomings in our civilization's dogged pursuit of a more perfect union.

This reality was all but confirmed by the experiences of French historian and political scientist Alexis de Tocqueville in the early 19th century. In his epic work *Democracy in America*, Tocqueville wrote, "Upon my arrival in the United States, the religious aspect of the country was the first thing that struck my attention; and the longer I stayed there, the more did I perceive the great political consequences resulting from this state of things, to which I was unaccustomed."[11]

He was unaccustomed to such a spectacle because unlike virtually all of its contemporaries, the

American nation benefitted from the active involvement of religious conviction in the public square.

As Tocqueville noted, "there is no country in the whole world in which the Christian religion retains a greater influence over the souls of men than in America, and there can be no greater proof of its utility, and of its conformity to human nature, than that its influence is most powerfully felt over the most enlightened and free nation of the earth."[12]

But if the church was indeed the great influence that led to political and social prosperity, would it not stand to reason that the church may bear a great deal of responsibility for our cultural collapse?

As the church goes, so goes the nation. Any diagnosis of what ails American culture must then realistically begin with an assessment of the status of the American church.

Sadly, such an assessment is not a pleasant exercise.

Depressing statistics about shrinking attendance, minister shortages, and the exodus of young people from the church may provide eye-catching graphs or attention-grabbing sound bites for those interested in a mere caricature of the problem. But, truth be told, those things are merely the logical outworking of the real crisis.

And the real crisis is a crisis of truth. One of the greatest Christian theologians of modern times, Francis Schaeffer surmised, "Here is the great [Christian] disaster – the failure of the [Christian] world to stand for truth as truth. There is only one word for this – namely, accommodation: the [Christian] church has accommodated to the world spirit of the age."[13]

If this is true, as it most certainly is...if we have blended our light with our culture's darkness...how will we ever convince them that they need to change?

If the church is to fulfill its responsibility as the conscience of America, a reformation is required. We must again hunger and thirst for righteousness, not accept superficiality masking itself as worship. We must crave enlightenment and grow weary of shallow entertainment.

Our reformation begins when the church once again finds the humility to accept, the willingness to embrace, the courage to defend, and the motivation to aggressively promote true Biblical Christianity.

CHAPTER FOUR

FIXED POINTS AND ROLLING ROCKS

Driving home from a tennis match my senior year of high school, I decided to turn on the radio. Though I had been a Christian for years, Christian stations were not programmed on the car dial. But as I scanned the channels that night, something prompted me to stop when I heard the squeaky voice of a Christian author and speaker named Frank Peretti who was being featured on one of Dr. James Dobson's Focus on the Family radio broadcasts.

It is not an exaggeration to say what I heard that night changed my life forever.

I had been raised in the church. I had excellent youth group leaders, wonderful Sunday School teachers, and ministers who spoke the Word of God boldly. And more than that, my parents had provided me a Godly home, read Bible stories to me every night, taught me to pray, and set my feet on the path that led me to the salvation I found in the nail-scarred hands of my Savior.

But this was different. That night in my old Chevy Cavalier, I was exposed – for the first time – to the concept of a Biblical Christian worldview. Peretti's words were so profound, I actually pulled into the parking lot of Sycamore Friends Church on my drive home, got my notebook out of my school backpack, and started feverishly writing down as much as I could catch.

I don't know the name of the speech Peretti was giving that night, but I still have those notebook papers. They have provided the basis for messages I have given, words that I have written, and the thinking that I proudly embrace. They are also the source for the remainder of this and the following most important chapters.

The 78 do not practice, and in many ways do not even fully understand anymore, Biblical Christian thinking. And without a reformation of thought to reclaim it, we – as individuals, families, church and society – are lost.

I did my undergraduate work at Indiana Wesleyan University, a small private liberal arts college, where I studied under a man named Dr. Glenn Martin. Dr. Martin was a brilliant thinker, himself dedicated to the resuscitation of Biblical Christianity in the culture. I took every class he offered, but my favorite was one called Western-American Intellectual and Social History (WISH). One reason I liked it was because just saying the name to people made me sound smart.

Perhaps a better way of describing the class would have been to just call it: "Hey Christians, you know what we believe and why, so here's what we don't believe and why." Not quite as academic a title, I suppose.

In this course, we studied about every religion and philosophy man has concocted for himself through the ages: from humanism to rationalism to transcendentalism to hedonism to romanticism to communism to utilitarianism to occultism…and about every other "ism" thrown in along the way. And what struck me as we went through this class was not the five notebooks worth of notes I compiled (though that has to be some kind of record), but the amazing pace at which man, throughout history, has invented new thought streams and philosophies to try to answer life's biggest questions in a way that allows him to escape the accountability of a sovereign God.

It is equally remarkable that as often as these worldviews of man freely transform with time and loosely blow with the wind of whatever is the day's prevailing sentiment, Biblical Christianity, by contrast, has not changed since it was first articulated.

In other words, as Peretti described it, Biblical Christianity has what all these other philosophies do not: a fixed point of reference.

The concept of a fixed point of reference is not overly difficult to grasp. When I was younger, my Dad took the family on one of his spectacular surprise vacations to Mammoth Cave in Kentucky. Yes, other kids were going to Disney World or Yellowstone…we went to a big hole in the ground.

But anyway, if you've ever visited Mammoth Cave, you know that the climax of your tour occurs once you've reached a large open room at the base of your descent. There, in the depths of the earth, the guides turn out all the lights that have been illuminating your passageways and tunnels. And it gets dark. Very dark. The guides tell you to put your hand in front of your face, and even when it is touching your nose, you can't see it.

Imagine in that pitch black environment being assigned to map out the large room where you're standing. Though it's a daunting task, it is possible even without light. In order to successfully accomplish it, you would first need to find some stable structure in the darkness that is permanent. Whether it's a rock formation or something man-made, if the object is immovable, it can serve as your reference point. From that fixed point, you can then measure out so many paces in one direction, so many in another until you've successfully mapped out the various elements and components of the room around you – even without the benefit of sight.

But what happens if that structure you are relying on begins to move? Obviously the moment that cornerstone becomes mobile, everything changes. Rolling the very rock that was to serve as your foundation around wherever you go will defeat your purpose. A fixed point of reference is only good if it exists apart from you and remains permanent...otherwise it is totally useless, and the false sense of guidance it offers is a danger to your safety.

Those who have ever attempted to navigate on open waters understand this reality. Before the days of

GPS tracking devices and other satellite guiding systems, explorers and fishermen relied on the stars as their system of navigation. Without such a fixed point on the horizon, their ships would drift off course and flounder at sea.

Is it any wonder then that from the very beginning, the Great Deceiver has sought to uproot our cornerstone and set humanity adrift in a sea of moral confusion? If his ultimate objective is to turn the hearts of men against God and thus destroy them, is there any more effective way of accomplishing it than by convincing man he is capable of navigating the treacherous oceans of life without a fixed point of reference? This was the exact strategy the serpent employed in the Garden of Eden.

There, God had presented man with heaven on earth. Man would want for nothing, and through his intimate relationship with his Creator, would have the perfect sense of moral discernment. But by appealing to man's pride, Satan poisoned the relationship between God and his crowning achievement and laid the philosophical foundation for virtually every false religion man has invented. Though many possess a superficial understanding of the "Fall of Man," what occurred in Genesis 3 requires a closer examination, as it exposes the toxic presuppositions that precipitate the totality of human suffering.

> Now the serpent was more crafty than any of the wild animals the LORD God had made. He said to the woman, "Did God really say, 'You must not eat from any tree in the garden'?"[1]

Notice the first thing Satan does is not to present himself as God's antithesis. He is not approaching Eve and demanding that she reject God explicitly and instead worship and trust him. He is merely calling into question the Word of God.

> The woman said to the serpent, "We may eat fruit from the trees in the garden, but God did say 'You must not eat fruit from the tree that is in the middle of the garden, and you must not touch it, or you will die.'"[2]

Eve, in answering the serpent's leading question, falls into his trap. In her response, she attributes words to God that He never spoke. In Genesis 2:17, God had indeed warned Adam not to eat of the tree of knowledge of good and evil (again, because by simply trusting God's care and provision, man had a perfect sense of good and evil), but God never told them they couldn't touch the fruit. Eve's response makes it clear that she sees God's prohibition as restrictive rather than protective. Recognizing this discontent, Satan then flatly contradicts God's Word:

> "You will not surely die," the serpent said to the woman.[3]

Once the groundwork for rebellion had been laid, Satan offered his fatal alternative. Understanding that in considering his overtures, Eve would undoubtedly wonder why her Creator would have lied about such an unnecessary rule, Satan slanders God's motives:

"For God knows that when you eat of it your
eyes will be opened, and you will be like God,
knowing good and evil."[4]

"You will be like God." With those five words,
Satan tore the cornerstone from its foundation and
ushered in the oldest religion in existence: humanism.
It is as if he said to Eve, "Once you eat the fruit, you
will be the god of your own little universe – you'll call
the shots, make your own truth, make your own reality.
You will determine for yourself what defines good and
bad, true and false." Such is the wicked temptation of
pride that has inspired countless world religions and
philosophies – each unique in their methodology and
theory, but all identical in their underlying
presupposition that ultimately, man is his own god.

And each of those philosophies has left behind
them a wake of destruction so large you would think
that by now we might have recognized the wisdom in
clinging to a fixed point of reference. But amazingly,
after thousands of years worth of history proving the
folly of allowing human intuition and passion to be our
moral compass, we appear as content as ever to wonder
aimlessly in the dark, relying on our own self-
determined truth to guide us.

Culturally, this fateful decision manifests itself
in moral confusion. It is exemplified in college
administrators who allow a man named Andrew
Martinez to walk around campus naked for months
because they fear offending his "rights of expression"
by telling him to put his clothes on.[5]

It is experienced in hospital corridors where in
one room you have an abortionist killing a full term

infant, while across the hall a team of prenatal paramedics prepare to rush in and save the life of the child if the abortionist fails.

Is it anything but society's moral confusion that says if you hold an infant's head inside the birth canal while inserting scissors and suction tips to extract its brain, you are completing a "legitimate medical procedure;" but doing the same thing with the infant's head outside the canal is first degree murder?

Is it not moral confusion for politicians to tout their refusal to "tell a woman what she can and can't do with her body," while simultaneously voting to ban salts, trans fats and high calorie fast foods? Evidently the sanctity of a woman's reproductive system is more secure than her digestive system.

The inconsistency further infects the minds of our leaders. When asked whether being "gay" was a choice, President Barack Obama responded, "I don't think it's a choice. I think that people are born with a certain makeup."[6] Other than being an unsubstantiated claim, how does this demonstrate moral confusion? Merely juxtapose that comment with another he gave during his first campaign for president. Asked when a baby gets human rights, Obama demurred, stating, "Answering that question with specificity, you know, is above my pay grade."[7] So the same man who claims he isn't enlightened enough to determine the humanity of what is conceived in the womb (something science unquestionably proves) simultaneously claims that he can determine the sexuality of what is conceived in the womb (something that science, to this point, disproves). That's confusion.

And it filters from the ivory towers of academia and the hallowed halls of the White House and Congress into our family rooms. It's what prompts a dad to call my radio show, with his son beside him, to challenge me on the notion of truth:

James: Hi Peter, thanks for taking my call. My son and I were sitting here listening to you talk about the existence of some be-all, end-all truth, and he actually said to me, 'that isn't possible.'

Peter: And did you agree with him?

James: I did. Because, you know, I've always tried to teach my kids that there are different ways of looking at the world and there are different perspectives people have and different paths that people take, and saying –

Peter: And each one of those perspectives and paths are equally valid?

James: And saying, well – and saying that this is a concrete right and this is a concrete wrong may be true given your perspective, but it's not maybe true given mine or my son's.

Peter: James, the last thing I'm trying to do is embarrass you in front of your son. I want you to know that. But, is this your approach to parenting?

James: What?

Peter: You have rules for your son, I'm sure.

James: Yes, I do.

Peter: And so say your son decides he doesn't like those rules. I'm sure he doesn't like some of them. And so he just decides not to follow them. Do you come down hard on him?

James: Yes, but that's different than what I'm talking about.

Peter: Actually, it's a pretty good test case. Why can't your son inform you that he has a different reality, a different set of standards, a different perspective than you? And to him, your rules don't make sense and aren't necessary?

James: Well, that's too bad for him then because I'm the dad.[8]

It's a classic response. But what is it? It is an authority structure torn free from any concrete moorings. "You do what I say because I said so." I suppose that works as long as your son is smaller and dumber than you. But James was breeding a real headache for himself as a dad in the long run as he attempted to stumble his way through the darkness of Mammoth Cave without anything to cling to. And worse, he was training his son to operate the same way.

The far better explanation of why dad's rules must be followed is an appeal to an absolute moral authority that set up the family structure, putting dad as the head of the household. Just as James is accountable to God for his actions, so James' son is accountable to his dad.

Our conversation went on, and it didn't get any more encouraging:

> Peter: So James, let's just take your thinking to its logical end. Can you answer a question for me? Who was a better person: Mother Teresa or Adolf Hitler?
>
> James: (laughing) Are you serious?
>
> Peter: Seriously, seriously. Who was a better person?
>
> James: (laughing) This is pretty easy to answer.
>
> Peter: Then answer.
>
> James: Mother Teresa was obviously a better person than Hitler. About anybody was better than Hitler.
>
> Peter: Okay, now tell me why.
>
> James: Mother Teresa spent her life caring for people and helping them. She was good. Hitler killed people because he was a dictator who wanted world power. How's that?

Peter: Not so good. Because do you realize, James, that Hitler was doing what he thought was right? He was merely speeding up the evolutionary process. He was attempting to bring about a master race and exterminate all the riff-raff. It's the same thing Planned Parenthood was founded to do. Get rid of all the lesser folks. Now, maybe you don't agree with his strategy, but he just had a different perspective on how to improve the lives of humanity than Mother Teresa, but ultimately they both wanted the same thing, right? So how can you determine Mother Teresa was better?

James: Because she didn't kill people.

Peter: Even better, why do you think it's better not to kill people? What if I said that it would have been more humane for Mother Teresa to kill all those impoverished people she lived with? Take them out of their misery! Why is this perspective wrong? You told me earlier we all have different perspectives.

James: Well, now you're just being, you're just, you're just playing games.

Peter: Actually I'm not, James. Because this goes to the heart of what I was just talking about. It proves the point I

was trying to make earlier perfectly.
Your call just made this segment for
me. For us, for all of us. You are
buying into, and you are teaching
your son to buy into a concept of
moral relativism that says there is no
truth. But it's self defeating. You
don't even believe it. I know that
because first, you called to tell me
what I was saying was wrong. Think
about that. The only way I can be
wrong is if there's some truth out
there to declare and prove my actions,
my words are wrong. But you say
that standard doesn't exist. And more
than self-defeating, it's dangerous.
There has to be a truth that is fixed,
that is right for all men, or we're in a
lot of trouble.

James: Well, you are saying that because you
are a product of your environment.
There is no such truth.

Peter: No truth? There is no truth?

James: Not in the sense that you're talking
about it.

Peter: So there is no truth. James, here's my
last question for you. You say there is
no truth. Is that true?

James: (nervous laughter) Nice try.[9]

I wasn't "trying" anything but to expose the faulty logic that is infecting the minds of so many Americans.

And most tragically of all, this moral incongruity has taken hold in our churches, where research indicates as little as 46% of American Christians actually believe in absolute truth that is consistent regardless of circumstances.[10] In other words, over half of American Christians are content to embrace the serpent's ideology: that we can be like God.

It's why I said earlier that even inside the walls of the church, remarkably few Christians have ever been confronted with – and even fewer grasp – and fewer still embrace – true Biblical Christianity. What we are preaching and teaching, and consequently breeding and reaping, is a humanistic version of have-it-your-way Christianity where man – not God – determines what is right. If the Bible goes along with our religion, we cite it. If it conflicts, we either ignore it or suggest it was never intended to be taken literally.

Such an approach is not Christianity, and those who condone it are not practicing Christians. Undoing their destructive subversion within the church will be difficult given the Biblical illiteracy of many self-professing believers. But it is a task most noble, and one that must begin with reestablishing the Christian worldview's fixed point of reference. Only then will we have hope of navigating through the darkness that surrounds us.

CHAPTER FIVE

PILLARS OF THE FAITH

When my dad left the U.S. Air Force active duty
and started going to law school, my family moved into
an old farmhouse next to my grandparents. The house
was over 100 years old and needed some major
renovating to even be livable. In fact, according to one
of the inspectors, "If the termites ever quit holding
hands, the house would probably collapse." But
despite these obvious concerns, all of the inspectors
gave a green light to our remodeling project for one
reason: the foundation was steady.

That is precisely why it is imperative for the
church to return to the firm foundation of Biblical
Christianity. For while the American church can
weather internal disagreements over style and method,
while it can survive the complicated wrangling over
doctrinal differences, a cracked or crumbling
foundation will usher in its destruction faster than any

other enemy. This was the concern embodied in the words of the Psalmist who wrote, "If the foundations are being destroyed, what can the righteous do?"[1]

Understanding this, it is not difficult to see why there are such concentrated and consistent attacks being waged against the fundamental pillars of Christianity. Those who seek to repeal and replace the Christian ethic of our culture know the most effective way of doing so is to systematically dismantle the belief system at its core. Break the rock loose from its props, and it no longer holds moral and rational superiority over all its meager intellectual competitors.

In order to stop this premeditated assault, the church must cease being obsessed with petty and childish distractions, and instead focus on restoring and buttressing its foundational pillars. It must again convey to a watching world that it possesses the answers to the deep questions of life. It must work tirelessly to demonstrate the supremacy of Biblical thought, teach the youngest generations to understand the significance of presuppositions, and champion the necessity of what Christianity alone offers…that fixed point of reference.

In the 17th chapter of the Book of Acts, we are confronted with the five pillars of that fixed point. All five represent critical and irreplaceable elements to the reformation upon which the survival of our culture depends. And perhaps as the result of divine providence, we find that the cultural circumstances we are experiencing today are not unlike those the Apostle Paul encountered when he first articulated this statement of Biblical Christianity.

According to Scripture, Paul (a former pious and learned Jew) spent the majority of his time reasoning and arguing with other Jews in their synagogues. He would use their common language and understanding of the Torah and Old Testament prophecies to make the case that Jesus Christ was their anticipated Messiah. But in Acts 17, Paul is speaking to a much different audience.

At the Areopagus, Paul was confronting Greeks who had never been to Sunday School. He was dealing with philosophers and thinkers who were foreign to the language of Jews and Christians. He was aware that though these men prided themselves on their wisdom and knowledge, he would have to begin reasoning with them from the most basic tenets of Biblical thought.

In our post-modern culture, we are no different. We must face the uncomfortable reality that entire generations have been raised apart from any firm grounding in Scripture. In the high school history classes that I teach, I am unable to reference key Biblical figures like Noah, Moses, King David or Solomon, because even the churched kids I have are unfamiliar with them.

I didn't know whether to laugh or cry one day teaching my senior government class when during a lecture on the history of law codes I mentioned Moses. Not wanting to embarrass anyone who didn't know the answer, I turned to a young man from my church and asked, "And what law code did Moses bring the world?" I was met with a blank stare. I tried to prompt him by saying, "They were carved on two stone tablets." The kid shook his head and said, "Well I know it's not the Constitution."

The foundations are indeed being destroyed. The ground is no longer fertile to bear the fruit of prosperity we have enjoyed for generations. It has become cracked and barren due to a lack of cultivation by those of us who were entrusted to its care. Consequently, we are in the same situation as Paul, speaking to an audience of those who must be confronted at the most basic, presuppositional level of thinking. May we find inspiration in the sacred words he wrote nearly 2,000 years ago.

PILLAR ONE:

> The God who made the world and everything
> in it...[2]

Notice the very first question that Paul, in speaking to the non-believers, addresses: the question of origins. Isn't it amazing that no matter who we are, where we're from, or what we believe, mankind struggles and grapples with these kind of fundamental questions? The Greeks certainly didn't believe in the Biblical God, and yet they were perplexed by the same question of origin that devout Jews and infant Christians were attempting to tackle.

And today is no different. A recent story from the science and environment department of BBC News reported on the mounting frustration many atheist scientists are experiencing over our inability to make contact with extra-terrestrial life somewhere in the universe.

The article quotes the father of the S.E.T.I. (Search for Extra-Terrestrial Intelligence) project, Dr. Frank Drake, as saying, "It's probably the most important question there is."[3] Admittedly, I find that statement beyond absurd. I can think of far more significant and pressing concerns to struggle with than whether E.T. is eating Reese's Pieces somewhere out in the cosmos.

It begs the question why someone as educated and intelligent as Dr. Drake would place such a premium on finding aliens. Why would he – as well as other prominent atheists like Carl Sagan – dedicate so much of their time, money and resources to such a cause? Once again, we find the answer begins with their presuppositions.

Men like Drake and Sagan are non-theists. They totally eliminate from consideration the very idea that God could have played any part in designing the universe. Consequently, if God did not make the world and everything in it (as Paul asserts), where did it all come from? This dilemma ironically leads boastful men like Drake and Sagan who reject the "irrationality" of seeking the Christian God, into a career obsession with finding Marvin the Martian.

While all men struggle to answer the question of origin, the atheist's presuppositions quite unscientifically arrest his thinking, forbidding any possibility outside the boundaries he concocts. These boundaries eliminate the Christian God from consideration, but not aliens.

Dr. Drake proudly explains, "What does it mean to be a human being? What is our future? Are there other creatures like us? What have they become? What can evolution produce? How far can it go? It will all come out of learning of extra-terrestrials and this will certainly enrich our lives like nothing else could."[4]

While they would be loathe to admit it, these evolutionary scientists – like the Greeks at the Areopagus – are frantically looking for meaning. They need answers to the big questions of life, and after having decided that those answers cannot come from any divine origin and purpose, they look for it anywhere they can find it...even if that means little green guys with antennas.

This explains then the sense of desperation they feel in not uncovering any evidence of such extra-terrestrial life. If they fail, that just adds yet another proof of the unique and special design of earth. The BBC article actually confirmed as much when the author concluded that maybe we weren't finding aliens because there weren't any out there: "The human race is either an accidental blip in the Universe or we are special and the conditions we evolved in were unique. The Rare Earth hypothesis argues that because of the intricate design and infrastructure of our planet, the amount of coincidences and circumstances that must occur together make life almost impossible."[5]

Impossible but for the intentional handiwork of a Grand Designer. The first pillar of the Biblical Christian Worldview rests on the first five words of the Bible: "In the beginning, God created."[6]

PILLAR TWO:

...is the Lord of heaven and earth...[7]

Even if we find an agreeable population when articulating the first pillar, we will inevitably encounter fierce resistance communicating the second. Agnostics doubt that God exists, but might be willing to concede the point if Christians agreed that's where God's dominion ended. Similarly, Deists believe that God created the world but then wandered off never to have further relationship with mankind. Other belief systems would be equally compatible with Christianity if it taught only that there was a God who designed all things and then left us in charge.

But as Paul makes clear, that is not what Christianity teaches. And that's where the philosophical conflict starts.

It is an incontrovertible fact of human existence that we don't like to be told what to do. Mankind struggles with authority. Whether it's children rebelling against their parents, parents resenting their bosses, or the masses resisting the government, the natural yearning of the human soul is freedom.

But just because we dislike authority certainly doesn't mean that authority doesn't – or shouldn't – exist. And in this brief, yet incredibly powerful statement to the Greeks, Paul is suggesting that there is an ultimate moral standard to the Universe. The Biblical God is more than just Creator. He is that fixed point of reference by which we measure good and bad, and to which all men will be held accountable.

Though moral behavior theories were espoused by those like Heraclitus and Plato, who predated Christ, the notion of a moral law or absolute truth met the same kind of objections then as it does today in our society.

After speaking at a church, a woman approached me and explained that though she had been a Christian most of her life, she had come to realize there simply could not be any concrete moral law. I asked her how she arrived at such a conclusion. She reasoned that if all people really know some fundamental code of right and wrong that has been written upon their hearts, as Scripture teaches, there simply wouldn't be such cruelty and evil in our world. This faulty logic is nothing new. Paul confronted it, and so must we.

To make such an argument, one must ignore the reality that the moral law tells us what ought to be done, not necessarily what is done. People willingly choose to suppress the moral law all the time. Even Paul told us in Romans that he was commonly guilty of such an offense. He wrote, "I do not understand what I do. For what I want to do I do not do, but what I hate I do...For I have the desire to do what is good, but I cannot carry it out. For I do not do the good I want to do, but the evil I do not want to do — this I keep on doing."[8]

In other words, the mere inability to follow the moral law does not disprove its existence, or the existence of the Moral Lawgiver. Put another way, it's not that there isn't a right to know, it's that we often don't have the strength to do what we know is right. In fact, had I thought about it, I would have expressed to this woman that her very ability to note the "wrong" that is done necessitates the existence of the very moral law she was denying.

Think about it. Whenever we are doing something wrong, we rationalize our behavior. As a teacher, I have heard some pretty remarkable explanations for why students have been cheating on exams. Why do they bother to concoct stories as wild as, "Well, my brother got his head caught in the microwave and we spent the night in the hospital, so I didn't have a chance to study?" Because they are attempting to justify something they know to be wrong. But how can they know that it's wrong apart from some moral authority?

Similarly, consider those who steal from the office. They say things like, "Well if they paid me what I'm worth, I wouldn't have to do this." Or think of those seeking vengeance that attempt to vindicate their actions by saying things like, "Well, he brought it on himself," or "He started it." Each one of those appeals for justification prove some ultimate sense of justice…the very position the Christian worldview attributes to the Biblical Creator.

Whether she realized it or not, this woman who approached me at the church was partially adopting a common atheist objection to the very existence of God. The atheist mind, shackled by its presuppositions, feebly asserts that if God truly exists, he must be malicious given all the injustice and cruelty that exists in the world. If he was loving, after all, he would prevent such brutality. C.S. Lewis, the brilliant Oxford scholar, exposed the assumption upon which this accusation rests – an assumption that contradicts and implodes the very argument being made.

Lewis questioned where the atheist derived his notion of cruelty and injustice, reasoning that one cannot know that a line is crooked if he has never seen a straight line. In other words, the only way for the atheist to accurately identify cruelty is if he has a standard of morality to compare it to. But that perfect standard is what the atheist is attempting to disprove. In a desperate effort to reject the notion of moral authority, his intellectual impotence actually ends up affirming its existence.

I witnessed this extraordinary phenomenon during an on-air debate back in November of 2007 with then president of American Atheists, Ellen Johnson:

> Peter: Now when you say you push for the ideals of atheism, or the standards, is it fair to say that atheism is a religion? You have morals and standards that you seek to advance, a belief system? Is that an appropriate term in your estimation?

> Ellen: No, we don't have morals or standards or a belief system. You know, it's, yeah, ethics are relative. Of course they are. Nothing is all black and white, and that's a good thing because life is not black and white.

> Peter: Well, what we have to be careful of is that we don't misinterpret the difference between moral truth and changing relativistic circumstances. For instance, I would encourage you to try to point out a society where running away in battle is looked at as an honorable thing. Or, beating someone is, assault and battery is looked at as an honorable thing.

There is a moral standard that exists across civilizations.

Ellen: Well there are religions that where in Saudi Arabia they beat the women, and that's a Muslim country. They beat the women.

Peter: Right. And you think that's wrong?

Ellen: Of course it's wrong.

Peter: Ok –

Ellen: But that's religion. And that's a religion that says that's okay.

Peter: It appears as though you have a moral standard by which you can tell those people what they're doing is wrong.

Ellen: And I'm an atheist.

Peter: Right.[9]

In those 30 seconds, Ms. Johnson wrecked the entire line of thinking she was espousing. After having passionately declared that all ethics are relative and that there is no black and white, she seemed pretty adamant that on the issue of beating women, it was fairly black and white.

It's the very type of intellectual corner atheists and humanists find themselves in whenever they call for any kind of evil to be eradicated and good to be done. By what standard do they measure those two things?

For instance, in a sign of their growing contempt for Christian thought, the American Humanist Association has apparently committed to making the Christmas season the backdrop for their annual membership drive. Punctuated by smart-aleck billboards and city bus placards, the AHA's banner slogan for the holiday season usually revolves around the catchphrase, "Why Believe in a God? Just be Good for Goodness' Sake."[10]

But the phrase "be good for goodness sake" is meaningless unless we can define what "goodness" is. For the believer, that is a relatively easy question to answer. Goodness is measured by the extent to which man's behavior conforms to the character and the will of his Creator. That is why the Christian believes the Bible is an irreplaceable component of human existence – its revelation serves to guide us towards that divine will.

But the atheist/humanist has no such moral center. They may talk at length about the need to be "good," but in the final analysis, their presuppositions fundamentally reject any concrete basis for morality.

That is not to say that anyone who is an atheist or humanist is a murderous butcher ready to pounce. Certainly there are a great number of nonbelievers who are benevolent, caring and kind. But while the atheist points to these upstanding godless citizens as proof of their theory that you can be good simply for goodness' sake, they conveniently ignore the cultural foundations that taught those individuals good from bad.

As columnist Jeff Jacoby observed, "In our culture, even the most passionate atheist cannot help having been influenced by the Judeo-Christian worldview that shaped Western civilization."[11] Put another way, the American atheist who boldly touts his morality and decency is humorously doing so only by appealing to the very Christian ethic they seek to denounce.

That is undoubtedly what happened during my debate with Ellen Johnson. Without thinking, she spoke the obvious: beating women is wrong. How does she know? Because the moral law written upon her heart has not been suppressed, but rather fostered and nurtured by the American culture in which she has been raised. That – whether she appreciates it or not – is what allows her the confidence to make such a firm statement of condemnation for those who abuse women.

This is exactly what C.S. Lewis was talking about when he wrote (my comments in italics):

> The moment you say that one set of moral ideas can be better than another (*like saying not beating women is better than beating women*), you are, in fact, measuring them both by a standard, saying that one of them conforms to that standard more nearly than the other. But the standard that measures two things is something different from either…You are, in fact, comparing them both with some Real Morality, admitting that there is such a thing as a real Right, independent of what people think, and that some people's ideas (*those who believe that beating women is wrong*) get nearer

to that real Right than others (*those who believe that it is okay to beat women*). Or put it this way: If your moral ideas can be truer, and those of the Nazis less true, there must be something — some Real Morality — for them to be true about.[12]

That "Real Morality" is, according to the second pillar of the Biblical Christian Worldview, the Creator God. Not just a designer, but the LORD over all things. The church must teach submission not just to the Saviorhood of Christ, but to His Lordship, as well. For if Christ is not Lord, neither will He be Savior. As my mentor, Dr. Glenn Martin, frequently asserted, "The Biblical Christian does not begin with man, but he begins with God, for God is Alpha and Omega; and if He is Alpha and Omega, He is everything in between as well."[13]

PILLAR THREE:

> ...and [he] does not live in temples built by human hands. And he is not served by human hands, as if he needed anything. Rather, he himself gives everyone life and breath and everything else.[14]

Listening to Frank Peretti that night in my car, one of his most compelling illustrations was this third pillar of the Biblical Christian Worldview: the self-defining and self-existing nature of God.

Peretti explained how the Greeks to whom Paul was speaking in this passage, had a funny way of working from the ground up. They would literally wake up on a given day and decide to build a new god. After pulling a large stone into the middle of the room, they would sit around and decide what kind of god they wanted. Concluding that they needed a fierce, fertile, and all-seeing god, they would promptly chisel muscles, sex organs, and eyeballs all over the rock, and then begin bowing down before it in worship.

I remember hearing Peretti's audience laughing at this thought. And I remember laughing myself given that this is such an obvious demonstration not of Greek mythology, but of the oldest religion in existence. The actions of the Greeks in this regard is the very nature of humanism: man creates, man reasons, man determines truth, man is god.

In this scenario, who created whom? The Greeks created their god. So what are they really worshipping? They are worshipping themselves – a projection of their own personality. They have determined the attributes of a god they deem worthy of their worship, they have created that object (even if only in their minds), and now they are worshipping it. Who then is really god in this situation? They are!

Knowing this habit of the Greeks, Paul is expressing to those gathered to hear the Biblical Christian Worldview that the God of Christianity is not like this. Paul expresses that the Christian God exists in and of Himself. He pre-existed man, and therefore does not need man to define Him. In fact, Paul stresses that the Christian God cannot be defined by man; indeed He is self-defining.

I remember thinking that God's answer to Moses at the burning bush was always peculiar. When Moses asked how to describe God to the Israelites he was being sent to deliver, "God said to Moses, I AM WHO I AM. This is what you are to say to the Israelites: 'I AM has sent me to you.'"[15]

I never really knew what that meant until I heard Peretti's explanation. You know you have reached the ultimate when that object is capable of self-definition. There is no way for a mortal mind to define the immortal God. He just is. The theological implications of such a revelation are immense. Nowhere else in the world do we find such a powerful claim about the nature of any god. This profound clarification demonstrates the impotence and feebleness of competing belief systems.

Right now in America it has become fashionable to make the claim that one is "spiritual" but not "religious." Many are flocking to what they see as the sophisticated nature of New Age spirituality in preference to the tired dogma of Christianity and "organized religion." Apparently, their communion of Starbucks lattes and rituals of Zen meditation are far more refined, as they sip Evian water and contemplate the big questions of life.

I've had the occasion of engaging a few of these New Age hipsters in conversation, and greatly enjoyed pointing out to them that far from being the progenitors of a bold, new faith, they had done nothing but embrace a retread version of humanism that Satan first articulated in the Garden of Eden. Not letting my "legalistic dogma" bring them down, they countered by asking me their favorite question (seriously, many of them spend hours upon hours discussing and debating this): "What's your definition of God, Peter?"

Thanks to that night with Frank Peretti, I'm always anxious to answer. "The answer to your question," I tell them, "is the very reason why you continue to spend inordinate amounts of time sitting here wasting your potential. The truth is that you don't define God and I don't define God. It is impossible for a mortal, finite human being to define or describe the immortal, infinite God. It is impossible for a meager human mind to put parameters around the identity of the omniscient Creator."

As they sit there pondering my statement, I go for the jugular: "It isn't up to man to define God because if man could define God, man would be God. Simply put, God is not a matter of your opinion. He is the great I AM WHO I AM, not the great I Am Whatever You Want Me To Be. God does not ask your opinion of Him and then morph and change Himself into meeting your expectations and preferences. Simply put: God isn't here to please you, He is here to be pleased by you and worshipped by you. Now, let me buy you that cup of coffee."

One of the reasons that those into New Age spirituality (which, again, is nothing more than a tired brand of humanism) struggle with this concept of a self-existing and self-defining God is because they see it as a repudiation of man's reason. Man is a thinking creature, and to say that there is an omnipotent God with all the answers, to them seems to render that reason unimportant and insignificant – something they cannot accept.

To the contrary, God has given man reason not to determine truth (if each of us could determine our own truth then ultimately there would be no truth) but to discover it as God has revealed it to us. Christians understand that discovering that truth is not always an easy task, and we really shouldn't expect it to be. Though God is the moral authority with a perfect sense of right and wrong, our fallen minds become corrupted with evil desires, temptations and emotions that can turn God's black and white into a muddy shade of gray.

Perhaps this is why we're reminded in Scripture, "For now we see through a glass, darkly; but then face to face: now I know in part; but then shall I know even as also I am known."[16] With our fallen vision it is sometimes difficult to see truth, but notice the key point this passage stresses: though we see through the glass darkly, we see through the glass. In other words, truth is knowable, it is discoverable, and it is applicable. That is the proper use of man's glorious reason, not sitting around in Starbucks attempting to determine what we think God should be like.

Because besides the mind-boggling arrogance it shows for the created being to attempt to judge the morality of his Creator, notice how this makes us no better than the Greeks that Paul was talking to at the Areopagus.

Consider as evidence two emails I received within the same week after having tackled the contentious issues of both homosexuality and abortion on my radio program. The first listener took me to task for condemning sexually depraved behavior by lecturing:

> I don't know what kind of Bible you're
> reading, but the God that I serve is a God of
> love. He loves people enough to die for them.

Do you really think he'd care who they slept with?

And less than a week later, from a different individual, I received this e-mail regarding my opposition to abortion:

> I'll tell you right now I don't know what kind of God you worship but he must be cruel. The God I worship believes that every person has the right to make decisions for themselves. The God I worship believes that a woman has a right to choose!

Or look at the words of Sister Helen Prejean, a devout opponent of the death penalty. In confronting Biblical evidence that supports the state's authority to carry out execution, Prejean famously responded to *Progressive* magazine, "I couldn't worship a god who is less compassionate than I am."[17]

These words demonstrate how similar Paul's audience at the Areopagus was to what surrounds us in the United States today. After all, what are these examples illustrating? They depict arrogant human beings determining the attributes of gods they deem worthy of their worship, then figuratively picking up their chisels, creating those gods and then bowing down before them.

Remember that the key to any fixed point of reference is that it is separate from you and immovable. Only in a self-existing and self-defining God, solely articulated as the third pillar of the Biblical Christian Worldview, do we find such a reliable cornerstone.

PILLAR FOUR:

> And He made from one man every nation of
> mankind to live on all the face of the earth,
> having determined their appointed times and
> the boundaries of their habitation.[18]

This fourth pillar of the Biblical Christian Worldview is the one that gives believers the basic understanding that there is something unique and sacred about human life. Such a concept has been all but totally rejected by our current post-modern culture.

To understand why, just consider what happens in the government school system every year. As students – churched and un-churched – fill biology and science classes, they are taught this one, fundamental, primary point about life: it is a total accident. Far from remaining neutral on the question of human origin, the government has embraced a state religion of humanism, and has proactively legislated that tax dollars will be used to cram it down the throats of every student.

Children are taught that it is scientific fact that human beings are nothing more than the meaningless conglomeration of molecules that came together purely by chance billions of years ago. I always find it beyond laughable when atheist social commentators like Bill Maher scoff at the Creation account as being irrational. As Maher and others mock the silliness of mystical gardens and talking snakes, I wonder if they have ever paused to consider that their alternative story is an even taller tale: that all the matter in the universe was at one point confined to a tiny pinpoint of light that one day decided to expand at a rapid rate.

This, we are told, set into motion a series of events that saw a bunch of dead, inorganic material look at itself and decide to just pop to life. Once alive, it formulated into a ball of goo, that eventually tired of being just goo and thus popped out legs. Following a few millennia, the goo-with-legs decided it would be neat to fly, and so it did. After tiring of flight, the creature flopped down to earth, hunched over and walked around as a monkey until it later stumbled across a razor, shaved, and became human. Pardon my cynicism Mr. Maher, but I think I'll stick with the Word of God over what Peretti accurately termed, "Goo to you by way of the zoo."

But this false teaching in our school system is not a joking matter. The consequences that come from teaching kids life is nothing but a cosmic accident, are deadly. After intellectually stripping humanity of its purpose and significance, our culture impotently offers "self-esteem" classes to try to help kids find the very meaning we have destroyed. Having convinced them that there is no Creator who holds the answers to mankind's existence, we idiotically counsel their natural bewilderment by telling them to "look within themselves" to find meaning.

But of course, we aren't God. And when those kids can't find the answers within themselves, many of them just choose to end their existence. And even those who don't have been poisoned with a lethal lie that when it fully manifests will destroy both them and the culture they have grown to control. They begin to view life as nothing but a mere product or machine part.

This is the socialist view of human worth: that there is nothing valuable about any one individual.

There's no spark of God's unique craftsmanship in every created being, but rather, man is a mere piece to fit into a puzzle. Or perhaps the better illustration is that of an engine.

For the purposes of full disclosure, I am admittedly missing that male testosterone chip that makes me really understand and appreciate automobiles. The old television sitcom *Frasier* once had an episode where the lead character Frasier and his equally un-masculine brother Niles had their car break down. They both fretted when someone suggested popping the hood because it might void the warranty. I'm not that bad, but I'm close.

Still, I know enough to know that an engine is made up of several working parts that must all be doing their role sufficiently for the engine to operate properly. This is the socialist view of society that we are coming to embrace in the United States. While there is nothing special about any one individual, we find our worth in serving the collective. This is the philosophy being bred in schools across America, and being reinforced by pop culture at every turn. So why is it a problem? Why is Biblical Christianity better?

Well, what happens when a certain engine part – say, a piston – breaks its connecting rod and no longer functions the way it was supposed to? When that happens we normally take our engine to the mechanic, and if he can't fix it, we throw that piston away and replace it. Once the piece is no longer serving the engine, it is of no use.

As this philosophy begins to take root in the United States, we are seeing our society begin to treat human life in the exact same way. When a certain part isn't serving us or functioning as it "should" anymore, we take it to the doctor. If he can't fix it, we discard that individual because they no longer serve the collective. Such is the logical basis for abortion, infanticide, euthanasia, doctor-assisted suicide, and every other life-destroying practice we are seeing explode with frightening regularity in our culture. As we continue perpetuating this evil thought stream, we move our society ever closer to the precipice of disaster. When we begin valuing human life for what it can do rather than what it is, catastrophe is not far off.

But Paul is giving us the alternative view in saying that "self-esteem" has nothing to do with self. In fact, the foundation of an individual's worth comes from the fact that he was made for a purpose, designed by a Creator who knew everything about him, and who formed him in the very image of God.

The significance of that point cannot be overstated. Dating back to the days immediately following the Great Flood, God made very clear that man was set above all living things. In the covenant with Noah, God put the most severe punishment in place for anyone who would destroy the life of a human being.[19] Why? Because that human being could do neat things? No. Because that human being is wanted and appreciated? No. But because that human being – all human beings – are made in God's image.

Imagine for a second what would happen if we started teaching kids that profound truth: that despite all your circumstances, difficulties, disabilities or struggles, you are made in the image of the Almighty who has a distinct plan and purpose for your life. And even when you feel the emptiest, remember that your life was worth the Creator's time in forming you and fitting you with an eternal destiny.

The transformative power of this fourth pillar of the Biblical Christian Worldview is what once made the United States the greatest defender of human rights the world has ever known. That's worth reclaiming.

PILLAR FIVE:

> God did this so that they would seek him and
> perhaps reach out for him and find him,
> though he is not far from any one of us.[20]

After laying out the first four pillars, Paul expresses one more powerful and spine-tingling principle that separates Biblical Christianity from all of its competitors. In its truest form, Christianity cannot properly be regarded as a religion. It's a relationship.

Religion is loosely defined as some institutionalized system of rituals and beliefs. And that encompasses every other world religion except Christianity. Yes, every religion is unique and different, but all of them have a common thread that is missing in Christianity.

In Judaism, man sets about the course of maintaining ancient customs, traditions and rituals to be able to maintain blessing and curry favor with God.

In Islam, man is called to acts of political conquest and subjugation to earn the blessing of Allah.

In Eastern religions like Buddhism and Hinduism, man dedicates himself to acts of meditation and contemplation to attain a higher level of consciousness with the gods...or in some cases to actually become a god himself.

Christianity is the only religion where man is not seen reaching up to God to try to attain to His realm. But rather, God, knowing the depraved state of mankind, knowing that man was totally incapable of redeeming himself, reaches down to deliver him. It is the only belief system that shows a God actively pursuing his Creation with a transcendent grace that prompts devotion motivated by love and thanksgiving rather than duty and obligation.

In this final pillar of the Biblical Christian Worldview, Paul confirms the mystery of the ages: that the Author of all things, who reigns as the Moral Authority over the universe, who self-exists as a transcendent being apart from his creation, who has taken the time to sanctify the gift of human life with His divine image…this same God wants us to know Him personally. He wants intimate fellowship with us, where our thoughts and ideas have been taken captive by His truth, and our beliefs and values begin and end with His authority.

These are the principles upon which we must stand. They are the pillars that have provided our civilization a fixed point of reference in navigating treacherous waters. They are the cornerstone for a reformation of thought that will once again transform the minds of our people to be able to distinguish between right and wrong.

This is the groundwork that must be preached from every pulpit and every lectern. Ministers who reject these principles must themselves be rejected as the false teachers and profiteers that they are.

Churches that fail to embrace and advocate these pillars must be abandoned and shuttered. They have lost their saltiness and are, "no longer good for anything, except to be thrown out and trampled underfoot."[21]

We cannot delay. The fate of the American nation depends on the fate of the American church. Let the reformation begin.

PART THREE
THE REVOLUTION

Politics are a part of a religion in a country as this, and Christians must do their duty to the country as part of their duty to God. He will bless or curse this nation according to the course Christians take to politics.

— *Charles Finney*

CHAPTER SIX

PRESERVING THE SACRED FIRE

Reforming the church is but the first step the 78 must take in saving our culture. Once this is undertaken, nothing short of a revolution of government will be required. Though this should go without saying, to save myself the headache, I will nevertheless stipulate that I'm speaking of an intellectual and philosophical revolution, not one marked by armed conflict.

In his celebrated Farewell Address, the father of our nation George Washington cautioned us against the destructive influence faction and party can have on a people. Rather than serving the general interest, Washington warned, the emergence of parties will elevate special interests above the good of the masses. This sectionalizing of the country would cause bitterness and misrepresentation to replace the brotherly kinship our Constitution sought to perpetuate. As he expressed his concerns about party loyalty ushering in the death of our nation, his words now seem frighteningly prophetic:

> You cannot shield yourselves too much against the jealousies and heart-burnings which spring from those misrepresentations; they tend to render alien to each other those who ought to be bound together by fraternal affection...To the efficacy and permanency of your Union, a government for the whole is indispensable.[1]

The idea of a "government for the whole" is a foreign concept in modern American politics. Every election cycle is met with the very type of pettiness and discord Washington lamented. Social classes are pitted against one another as class warfare becomes an effective vehicle for unscrupulous men to garner votes. Races are exploited; religious groups are demonized; certain occupations or industries are elevated as "too big to fail," and thus more important than others; all this stirs up the "jealousies" and "heart-burnings" that characterize a nation being torn apart at its seams.

And that isn't all. Statesmen who once reluctantly agreed to serve in a position of public trust have been replaced with politicians who will spend small fortunes to attain, and destroy anyone who stands between them and the power of high office. Have we paused long enough to consider why?

Is it perhaps because the corrupting nature of power is far more tempting today since our government has grown well beyond its intended size? Is it perhaps because having abandoned the

Constitutional limitations of government authority, those in power have the frightening ability to do as they please with little popular recourse? Is it perhaps because government office is no longer marked by burdens and obligations, but rather perks and privileges? Is it perhaps because the expectation of governing is no longer about the responsibility to protect people, but about the opportunity to dole out favors and accrue great wealth?

All of these answers play a part in explaining our current predicament, and demonstrate why we so desperately need a total revolution of the governing philosophy in America. Campaigns for elective office should not be characterized – as they currently are – by a competition of who can promise the most things to the most people. Those in positions of public trust should serve the general population responsibly rather than deflecting resources and gifts to particular regions or groups that are critical to their re-election bid.

Whenever I make such assertions, I am immediately called an idealist who doesn't understand the nature of politics. To the contrary, I do understand the nature of our politics and therefore recognize the change that so desperately needs to occur.

It may seem idealistic and foolish to say that our political leaders should give the people the kind of government they want. After all, there are 300 million different people in the country, with different ideas, different desires, different dreams, and different needs. Conservatives won't be pleased with a left-leaning government, liberals won't be pleased with a right-leaning government, and compromising somewhere in the middle will just make everyone unhappy.

But far from undermining my thesis, this reality proves my point. As respected pollster Scott Rasmussen correctly observes, "The American people don't want to be governed from the left, the right, or the center. The American people want to govern themselves."[2] Rasmussen is right. Americans have always craved self-government.

This concept has been woven into the fabric of our civilization from the day the Pilgrims landed at Plymouth. Before departing their ship, they crafted the first form of self-government in the new world – the Mayflower Compact – and then embarked on the grand experiment of self-rule that would come to define their descendents. From Locke to Lincoln, early influences on American governing thought all revolved around the same concept: that while submission to government may be necessary for social order to prevail, the human soul will find contentment only when that submission yields liberty, rather than denies it.

Let man govern himself and he will be more productive, more industrious, more charitable, more profitable, more generous, and more useful to society than by ruling over him.

This has been the crucial distinction that made the American Constitutional order and system a novelty in the political world, and the envy of nations. Nowhere else has the individual autonomy of man been held in such high esteem. Indeed, man's natural yearning for freedom was regarded as an annoying obstacle for the autocrats and monarchs of the past.

But the architects of American government began with a boldly unique premise. They started out with the assumption that man's natural state is freedom. Enshrined in our founding document, the Declaration of Independence, are those immortal words:

> We hold these truths to be self-evident, that all men are created equal, that they are endowed by their Creator with certain inalienable Rights, that among these are Life, Liberty and the pursuit of Happiness. — That to secure these rights, Governments are instituted among Men, deriving their just powers from the consent of the governed.[3]

And with those words, government in America became not an institution that grants man his liberty, but rather an institution man creates to protect his liberty. In other words, liberty pre-exists government. This monumental change in philosophy fundamentally altered the relationship between man and the state. For the first time, it made man autonomous and responsible for himself and his own happiness.

Notice that the Declaration guarantees only a right to pursue happiness, not a guaranteed right of happiness. Why? Because the architects of our Republic didn't want us to be happy? Hardly.

Our Founders wisely understood that happiness, contentment, security, and blessing are not the same for every individual. What brings me happiness may be – and likely is – something entirely different than what brings you happiness. So, the Founders reasoned, it would be impossible for any government to reasonably guarantee its people happiness because there would be no way to know, grasp, and fulfill every individual's personal definition of that word. People are simply too different and too unique. If you doubt that conclusion, let me challenge you to simply open your eyes and look around.

When I was much younger I remember watching some of the L.A. riots on the news. Many of those scenes of complete social upheaval are forever burned into my mind's eye, particularly one image I will never forget. As looters were carrying all kinds of electronic equipment, musical instruments, food and luxury items through the burning streets, the camera panned over and caught a shot of a man running out of the front window of a decimated furniture store. As he sprinted as fast as his legs would carry him, he wore a grin from ear to ear that signified his belief that he had just hit the mother load. I did a double take when I finally made out the object he'd stolen that had apparently brought him so much pleasure. Underneath both of his arms he was carrying two bright yellow, vinyl bean bag chairs. Totally oblivious to the fact that everyone else was carrying television sets, he was perfectly content with his canary cushions.

Though I can't imagine ever participating in riots, I can assure you that if I did, I'd pass on the vinyl bean bag chairs. But for this man, they were everything. In other words, he and I are different.

Or even consider those a bit closer to me. My wife and father-in-law are obsessed with running mini-marathons. I don't understand it. I cannot fathom how anyone can find joy in waking up at 4:00 in the morning, driving an hour and a half in the darkness, standing in subfreezing temperatures until they finally allow you to start running…for 13.1 miles. And they want you to pay them for the opportunity to do so! In the sports I played, running was a punishment. But for some people – even people I share many other interests with – they find happiness in what would be my misery.

And I could keep going: people who like to board large metal death tubes and slice through the air at 30,000 feet, people who spend money on electrical shock devices to hook up to their stomachs in the hopes of getting in shape through electrocution rather than exercise, people who like to jump off of bridges with a rubber band tied to their feet – none of those things come close to what I would call happiness. But for others, they are indispensable pleasures that they couldn't live without.

If that's the case, let me again ask how any government can possibly guarantee happiness to such an eclectic array of individuals? It simply can't; and our Founders wisely recognized that reality. They knew that there was no way any governing authority – no matter how big it was – could possibly fulfill every individual's passions and interests. And so instead, they did something ingenious.

They said in essence, "We will acknowledge that every man has the right to pursue whatever happiness is for him. We will create an environment of freedom and liberty where we will unleash the individual brilliance of man to a greater degree than has ever been done before. We will let him start businesses, run those businesses, invest, save, plan, work, labor, play, and do whatever he wants to do with little interference from governing authority."

In America, government was not designed to run people's lives while granting them some freedom along the way. Rather, people ran their own lives and granted government some important responsibilities to fulfill along the way. This stood the old system on its head. Thomas Jefferson acknowledged as much when he wrote, "When forced to assume [self-government], we were novices in its science. Its principles and forms had entered little into our former education."[4]

Their radical departure from the past is also why the American experiment was subjected to such ridicule and derision from those who anticipated its quick demise. Our trans-Atlantic foes simply saw no reason to believe that man, when left to his own devices, could possibly fulfill all the necessary tasks and duties associated with a growing and prosperous society.

Over 230 years later, it would seem safe to say that they were proven wrong. The revolutionary ideas in the American Declaration of Independence gave birth to the most blessed, the most prosperous, the most talented, the most advanced, and the most envied civilization in world history. And why? Because the government got out of the way and let man self-govern and pursue his dreams.

In his historic visit to the United States, Alexis de Tocqueville marveled at that reality, observing,

> Americans of all ages, conditions, and dispositions constantly unite together. Not only do they have commercial and industrial associations to which all belong but also a thousand other kinds, religious, moral, serious, futile...Americans group together to hold fetes, found seminaries, build inns, construct churches, distribute books...They

establish prisons, schools by the same method
... I have frequently admired the endless skill
with which the inhabitants of the United
States manage to set a common aim to the
efforts of a great number of men and to
persuade them to pursue it voluntarily.[5]

With such a legacy of prosperity and success, it
would seem impossible that the treasured principles of
the Declaration could meet with any objection today.
How, given the remarkable achievements and
accomplishments resulting from the American
experiment with self-government, can anyone
legitimately oppose the unfettered embrace of human
liberty and personal autonomy?

The answer is fairly simple: tyranny is timeless.
The effort to undermine and subvert liberty while
controlling and manipulating the individual through
expanding the state has been going on for ages, and it
continues today. And what is most dismaying is that in
recent decades, the effort has gained much traction in
our culture by making emotional appeals that fool
those who have become complacent in their
appreciation for American exceptionalism.

For instance, those who war against individual
freedom rarely do so by directly announcing their
intentions. They don't state their desire to strip people
of their ability to pursue happiness. Rather, they
simply lament what might occur if that pursuit was left
un-regulated and un-manipulated by the state.

What if people fail? What if they fall through
the cracks? What if they don't succeed? What if their
businesses collapse? What if they make unwise
investments? What if they lose their homes? What if

they can't afford college?

Well, the reality is that in a free society, those things will happen. There's no question that the freedom to succeed means the freedom to fail. And that's what this movement, found on the political left, deems unacceptable. "We can't let them do that! We must take care of them!" No, you don't...for two primary reasons.

First, Americans have always done a better job than anywhere else in the world at taking care of each other. It's where that miraculous interaction between virtue and free markets, morality and economic liberty, Christian principle and prosperity takes place.

And second, because the only way to effectively prevent failure is to simultaneously prevent success. In order to stop someone from making an unwise investment or a bad business decision, you must stop them from making any investment or business decision on their own. You must thwart their ability to take risks, because with risk comes the possibility of failure.

But have we forgotten how productive failure is to any vibrant society? Without failure, we don't know what things not to do. Attempting to find a millionaire who has never failed is a futile task. That should tell us something.

In any effort to prevent failure, the government must strip people of their individuality, autonomy and independence, treating them as chattel slaves...mere pawns in the hands of those in authority.

It's been done before...repeatedly...and with tragic consequences. Central planners fail not because they are evil, but because as we've said, people are too different, unique, and have too widely varying skills and needs to be manipulated into happiness by a top-down government bureaucracy. No matter how wise, well-intentioned, or intellectual our leaders may be, they simply cannot plan our lives better for us than we can do for ourselves.

The imminent French statesman and classic liberal theorist Frederic Bastiat explained why:

> To tamper with man's freedom is not only to injure him, to degrade him; it is to change his nature, to render him, insofar as such oppression is exercised, incapable of improvement; it is to strip him of his resemblance to the Creator, to stifle within him the noble breath of life with which he was endowed at his creation.[6]

For proof, simply visit an Indian reservation. This is a perfect example of what happens to a people who are stripped of their ability to self-govern and instead are "taken care of" by those who seek to prevent their failure. Given billions of dollars every year to improve the lives of Indians, the government has created the most destitute, impoverished, miserable people among us.

Our founders wisely understood that lesson. They weren't perfect men. But they understood that no men were perfect, and therefore the idea of giving a small contingent of imperfect men all powerful dominion over the masses wasn't a recipe for happiness. It was a recipe for misery and tyranny. They understood it, because they lived it.

It's why they chose a different direction for us. It's why George Washington proclaimed in his first

inaugural address that, "the preservation of the sacred
fire of liberty [is] finally staked, on the experiment
entrusted to the hands of the American people."[7]

 And it becomes incumbent upon us, the 78...the
ones who by virtue of our Biblical Christian Worldview
understand the brilliance and unique nature of man
and his God-given individuality to a greater degree
than anyone else in our culture, to rise up and defend
it. When we do, we will ensure that the experiment is
preserved and the sacred fire continues to burn.

CHAPTER SEVEN

THE ENEMIES OF FREEDOM

In a 2010 interview with MSNBC's Tom Curry, I commented that while our military is called to protect us from the enemies of freedom that are foreign, we citizens have the solemn responsibility of being on guard against those enemies of freedom that are domestic.

I think Tom missed my point. In his article he wrote, "For Heck, 'enemies of freedom' means [President Barack] Obama, [Speaker Nancy] Pelosi and [Democrat Representative Joe] Donnelly."[1] He apparently concluded that mine was nothing but a shallow, rhetorical, political attack on Washington Democrats that I didn't want to see keep their jobs. But it was more than that.

In order to defend the unique American experiment in human liberty and secure the dignity of individual man that it guarantees, we must be shrewd enough to recognize the threats against it. Our natural inclination is to believe that freedom's enemies are those who aggressively assail it in broad daylight. We look for the march of imperial dictators, or the rise of totalitarian regimes. And certainly those forces represent a danger that cannot be ignored.

But in the infant days of our Republic, the Father of the Constitution James Madison wisely cautioned us that such aggression is a secondary hazard when compared to another sinister enemy of freedom that lurks in the shadows. He wrote, "Since the general civilization of mankind, I believe there are more instances of the abridgement of freedom of the people by gradual and silent encroachments by those in power than by violent and sudden usurpations."[2]

In other words, sometimes the most serious enemies of freedom are not those that come in spectacular scenes of exploding airliners and smoldering buildings, but instead are those that come from within. They come with a smile and a promise to make our lives better if we will but yield just a little bit more of our freedom to them. They promise to even the playing field, ensure equality, and promote fairness if we just entrust them with more of our earnings, our resources, our autonomy and power. And when we do – when we are ensnared by their deception and willfully exchange our self-reliance for dependence upon them – we find that we have forged our own chains.

A diligent student of government, Madison noted that, "If we go over the whole history of the ancient and modern republics, we shall find their destruction to have generally resulted from those causes."[3]

So naturally, protecting against this insidious threat to self-government was a primary concern our Founders carried into the Constitutional Convention of 1787. In what may be the finest explanation of the delicate balancing act they were attempting in dividing authority and diffusing power, Madison stated,

> If men were angels, no government would be necessary. If angels were to govern men, no internal controls on government would be necessary. In framing a government which is to be administered by men over men, the great difficulty lies in this: you must first enable the government to control the governed, and in the next place oblige it to control itself.[4]

Here, Madison is identifying the two primary dangers in sustaining any experiment in self-government: licentious and unscrupulous men (lawless men), and those wielding power over others (law men). As counterintuitive as it may seem to us today, he and his fellow Founders believed that human liberty faced a graver threat in the latter than in the former.

They had experienced the consequences of the consolidation of power and distrusted any system that placed too much of it in the hands of a select few. It's why Madison authored our grand charter with the opening words, "We the People," and why 76 years later Lincoln would champion government of, by, and for the same. They were fierce defenders of the idea that the best way to prevent the abolition of God-given human liberty was by making man his own government to the greatest degree possible.

Jefferson wrote, "Sometimes it is said that man cannot be trusted with the government of himself. Can he, then, be trusted with the government of others? Or have we found angels in the form of kings to govern him? Let history answer this question."[5]

In other words, if we aren't going to trust man to take care of himself, why would we entrust him with the power to take care of others? Jefferson, in particular, despised the haughty attitude of nobility who believed themselves to be of greater pedigree than the peasants beneath.

It's one reason why as President, Jefferson humorously made it a habit to answer the White House door in his pajamas whenever foreign kings and queens came to visit. Though appalling to heads of state who saw themselves too dignified to be greeted in such a manner, Jefferson was sending a message: in America, we do things differently. Those in power are nothing more than commoners who have been temporarily entrusted to oversee certain tasks and duties the people cannot do for themselves. And even more significant, governing officials do not wield power indefinitely, but rather serve at the pleasure of those people.

There was no questioning the fear our Founders had of the tyrannical designs of those in power. It's what caused them to warn so often and so aggressively about the need for eternal vigilance in resisting the temptation to exchange freedom for a false promise of protection. As Benjamin Franklin famously quipped, "Those who would give up essential Liberty, to purchase a little temporary Safety, deserve neither Liberty nor Safety."[6]

The wisdom inherent in that admonition explains why our Founders repeatedly considered their creation of the world's first republic built upon the concept of self-government to be an experiment. Whether their posterity could recognize and ward off these threats posed to human liberty would determine its success or failure. Some, like Jefferson, expressed great confidence in our ability to do so, writing, "Those who will come after us will be as wise as we are, and as able to take care of themselves as we have been."[7]

Are we? Have we guarded against the temptation to surrender our essential liberties to purchase a little temporary safety? Have we resisted the deadly exchange of self-reliance for dependence? Have we consistently favored freedom even in the face of failure? Or have we begun entrusting into the hands of the few the very power that was so wisely reserved for us? Have our governing institutions become our masters? Have we forged our own chains?

Though perhaps an uncomfortable exercise, the best way of measuring our success or failure is to return to our founding document, the Declaration of Independence. Too often, we forget that the Declaration is the fundamental basis of Americanism. In celebrating with great reverence the wisdom of the U.S. Constitution, we lose sight of the fact that the Declaration embodied the underpinnings of its grand design. The Constitution created a system to enact, protect, and promote the principles of good government that were expressed in the Declaration.

But if the Declaration of Independence reveals what good government looks like, it will also tell us the type of government we should abhor, guard against, and find intolerable. In fact, that is what the majority of the Declaration involves. After his soaring philosophical opening that expounds upon the Natural Rights of all men, Jefferson settles in for a compelling critique of the King of England's tyrannical abuses.

This lengthy section, commonly known as the list of grievances, should not be glossed over or considered merely a rote recitation of complaints that were germane only to the American colonies in the late 1700s. These are the actions of a government that our Founders believed demanded a revolution to correct.

Compare them to the current realities of American government today and you see why the 78 must be demanding the same.

> He has called together legislative bodies at places unusual, uncomfortable, and distant from the depository of their Public Records, for the sole purpose of fatiguing them into compliance with his measures.

The enactment of the Patient Protection and Affordable Care Act of 2010 (popularly known as ObamaCare) creates at a minimum 100 new bureaucracies through which the personal health decisions, costs, approval and payment of individuals will be facilitated and managed. Wish to complain about a decision? Take a number and have a seat.

> He has erected a multitude of New Offices...

In 2009 alone, the United States federal government saw the naming of nearly 30 unelected "czars" to wield oversight and statutory power over the people and their interests.[8]

> ...and sent hither swarms of Officers to harass our people and eat out their substance.

Following the passage of the new healthcare law, Representative Kevin Brady of Texas released the findings of a Joint Economic Committee and House Ways and Means Committee minority report that estimated up to 16,500 new IRS agents would be needed to "collect, examine and audit new tax information mandated on families and small businesses" as a result of the legislation.[9] Another way of saying that would be "swarms of officers engaged in harassment of the people."

> He has combined with others to subject us to a jurisdiction foreign to our constitution, and unacknowledged by our laws; giving his Assent to their Acts of pretended Legislation.

At the end of his term in December 2000, then President Bill Clinton signed the Rome Statute, aligning the United States with the authority of the International Criminal Court.[10] Wide ranging ICC influence would allow foreign governments to try Americans for what they deem "atrocity crimes."

And in recent years, great efforts have been made by American government officials to subject the United States to an international climate agreement that would arbitrarily – and without recourse – limit the energy usage of American businesses and citizens.

For imposing taxes on us without our
Consent.

Though Americans today enjoy the benefit of
representation that our revolutionary ancestors were
denied, it is absurd to suggest that we have willfully
consented to the myriad of taxes, fees, levies and duties
placed upon virtually every aspect of our existence.

Even a cursory survey of the tax burden of
modern Americans, including the accounts receivable
tax, alternative minimum tax, automobile registration
tax, building permit tax, capital gains tax, cable TV tax,
CDL license tax, cigarette tax, corporate income tax,
court fines, dog license tax, electricity tax, estate tax,
federal income tax, federal unemployment tax, fishing
license tax, food license tax, fuel permit tax, gasoline
tax, grocery tax, hunting license tax, inheritance tax
interest expense, inventory tax, IRS interest charges (tax
on top of tax), IRS penalties (tax on top of tax), liquor
tax, local income tax, luxury tax, marriage license fee,
Medicare tax, parking tax, personal property tax, real
estate tax, septic permit fee, service charge taxes, sewer
tax, Social Security tax, road usage tax for truckers,
sales tax, recreational vehicle tax, road toll booth tax,
school tax, sin tax, state income tax, state
unemployment tax, telephone federal excise tax,
telephone federal universal service fee tax, telephone
federal, state and local surcharge taxes, telephone
minimum usage surcharge tax, telephone recurring and
non-recurring charges tax, telephone state and local tax,
telephone usage charge tax, toll bridge tax, toll tunnel
tax, trailer registration fee, utility tax, vehicle license
registration tax, vehicle sales tax, water tax, watercraft

registration tax, well permit fee, workers compensation tax, reveals at least a few that must be considered as the product of unwanted imposition.

> [For] Obstructing the Laws for Naturalization
> of Foreigners...

After cramming through blanket amnesty for nearly 3 million aliens who broke the laws of immigration and naturalization in 1986, there continues to be strong interest amongst governing officials to do it again today. This time, such amnesty would involve approximately four times the original amount, as up to 12 million illegal immigrants would be given preferential treatment and a "pathway to citizenship" over those who have patiently and faithfully sought entrance legally.

> He has forbidden his Governors to pass Laws
> of immediate and pressing importance, unless
> suspended in their Operation till his Assent
> should be obtained; and when so suspended,
> he has utterly neglected to attend to them.

Have we been watching what is going on at the border? Because of the abject failure of our federal government to stop the spreading violence associated with illegal immigration along our southern border, the state of Arizona took action in 2010 to protect itself.[11] The state's governor signed legislation giving state law enforcement the ability to assist the federal government in cracking down on illegal immigration.

But rather than support Arizona in their efforts to protect its citizens who are dying as a result of the lawlessness (what many would consider an issue of "pressing importance"), President Barack Obama's administration successfully filed and fought a lawsuit against the state, forbidding them from enacting their law.[12] And after suspending their efforts indefinitely, the federal government has continued utterly neglecting the problem.

> He has endeavored to bring on the
> inhabitants of our frontiers, the merciless
> Indian savages, whose known rule of warfare
> is an undistinguished destruction of all ages,
> sexes, and conditions.

There can be no more appropriate words to describe the behavior of the Mexican drug cartels that have now taken over large swaths of land in the American southwest than these: merciless beatings, savage destruction of the lives and properties of ranchers, farmers, and families. And yet in spite of the terror, in spite of the fact that county sheriffs in the area have claimed, "Mexican drug cartels literally do control parts of Arizona,"[13] the only response from our government – those with the sworn duty to protect the lives of their fellow citizens – has been to place signs along the interstate warning travelers of armed drug and alien smugglers.

Merely posting signs that acknowledge an "active drug and human smuggling area" characterized by "armed criminals and smuggling vehicles traveling at high rates of speed,"[14] and cautioning travelers to use other routes, doesn't solve the problem. In fact, lack of action only invites more trouble.

He has kept among us, in times of peace,
Standing Armies...

Though it hasn't yet been realized, consider this alarming quote from President Barack Obama during his campaign for office in July of 2008: "We cannot continue to rely on our military...We've got to have a civilian national security force that's just as powerful, just as strong, just as well-funded."[15]

Altering fundamentally the Forms of our Governments. For suspending our own Legislatures, and declaring themselves invested with power to legislate for us in all cases whatsoever.

Whether it was President George W. Bush pushing through the largest expansion of the federal government's reach into the realm of education – an area where the federal government has no constitutional authority to act, or President Barack Obama signing a Congressional mandate forcing citizens to engage in commerce by purchasing health insurance, leaders of both political parties seem committed to usurping the power that was never intended for the national government, but rather reserved to the states.

By doing so, they fundamentally reshape the nature of our government to one the Constitution does not prescribe.

In every stage of these Oppressions We have
Petitioned for Redress in the most humble

terms: Our repeated Petitions have been
answered only by repeated injury.

These words embody a perfect encapsulation of
the feelings of millions of angry constituents who have
written, called, faxed, and begged their Congressmen to
oppose a litany of big government policies that
Washington has used to regulate everything from
liposuction to marijuana to school vending machines.

Despite our most stringent objections, the tone
deafness of the American ruling class has become epic.
That is why our response must be equally ambitious.

On the night the Democrats in Washington
passed the ObamaCare bill through the House of
Representatives, then Speaker of the House Nancy
Pelosi gave a spine-tingling speech. In it, she
proclaimed that by expanding the federal government
to unprecedented size, she and her comrades were
fulfilling the words of our Founders (men who went to
extraordinary lengths to expound upon the need for a
small government of limited scope).[16]

The truth is that Pelosi was right. The actions of
our current leadership class in Washington are
fulfilling the words of the Founders – the words they
used in the Declaration of Independence to depict bad,
destructive and oppressive government.

If we seek to preserve the blessings of liberty to
our posterity, we must acknowledge that our
government today is coming to eerily resemble not the
kind our Founders created…but the kind they pledged
their lives, their fortunes, and their sacred honor to war
against.

CHAPTER EIGHT

THE BULLY'S PLAYGROUND

Human liberty, as great as it is, is not enough.

For the last two chapters, I have written about the Founders' insistence upon respecting the autonomous nature of man and freeing him to self-govern. But freedom alone is not sufficient in producing a happy and prosperous society. It is why I do not consider myself a libertarian, despite the high premium I place on individual liberty.

For those to whom liberty is the ultimate value, the starting and ending point of existence, they fail to note a somber reality of which our Founders were keenly aware: freedom, un-tempered by responsibility is a destructive – not productive – force.

Reflecting on the horror of the French Revolution, classic political theorist Edmund Burke wrote, "What is liberty without wisdom, and without virtue? It is the greatest of all possible evils, for it is folly, vice, and madness, without tuition or restraint."[1]

Unfettered freedom breeds chaos. And a lawless society – or one without a firm foundation for law – is self-destructing. In other words, there is a secret about the success of self-government that separates those who reap its blessings from those who suffer from anarchy and unbridled passions. Our Founders understood the linchpin that held a free society together, and they went out of their way to teach and transmit it to us. It is our responsibility to listen.

During the presidential election of 2008, professing Mormon candidate Mitt Romney gave a much-anticipated speech on religion in American politics. In the course of his address, Romney made an insightful – if not in our day, controversial – remark: "Freedom requires religion just as religion requires freedom."[2]

Atheists around the world came unglued. One such atheist, Christopher Hitchens, railed against Romney's declaration, bellowing, "Any fool can think of an example where freedom exists without religion – and even more easily of an instance where religion exists without freedom."[3]

For supposedly deep thinkers, atheists like Hitchens have an amazing propensity for making shallow observations appear like profound contemplations. Because oddly enough, after proclaiming that any numbskull could do it, Hitchens failed to cite any such example to prove his point.

In fairness to him, Hitchens is right about the latter part of his statement. There are multiple world religions that do not encourage freedom, but rather condemn it. One need only travel to the Middle East and witness the oppression of women, the limitations on dissent, and the refusal to allow any participation in religions besides Islam to grasp this. Romney's statement would have been more appropriately phrased, "Freedom requires a moral law, just as a moral law demands freedom."

Hitchens would have been grasping at straws to refute such an observation. He would not only have been taking on Romney, but the entire company of America's Founders as well. In fact, Romney's was nothing more than a repackaged sound bite version of the collective views of some of history's foremost thinkers on human liberty.

The most underrated American patriot, John Adams, penned the words, "We have no government armed with power capable of contending with human passions unbridled by religion and morality."[4]

What does that mean? It means that no government is big enough to stop crime and make people treat each other the right way. Yes, it can punish misbehavior. But government punishment, as necessary and as motivating as it may be, is reactive...it takes place after the crime has been committed. Adams' sober words then are cautioning us that any experiment in self government depends upon the people possessing an internal moral restraint.

Without such personal virtue, Adams warned, freedom will turn deadly:

> Avarice, ambition, revenge, or gallantry, would break the strongest cords of our Constitution as a whale goes through a net. Our Constitution was made only for a moral and religious people. It is wholly inadequate to the government of any other.[5]

Those words, if spoken today, would generate the ire of both the secular humanist left and the libertarian crowd, who would accuse their author of some diabolical scheme to shackle the country with a right-wing religious code of behavior. But Adams was not some theocratic nut who was attempting to force people into the baptistery through the force of law.

He simply recognized that Christian principle teaches moral restraint. And since moral restraint is the linchpin to the success of a free society, he acknowledged that apart from it, the U.S. Constitution alone would be unable to sustain the American experiment in self-government.

If Hitchens or others struggle to grasp this point, they should consider what the intervening 230 years have demonstrated. At the time of our founding, America had no drug laws, gun laws, child labor laws, or minimum wage laws. Why didn't they? Because our ancestors believed in child labor or mistreating the working man? Because they were gun-toting stoners? Of course not. They didn't have these laws because they didn't need them.

A common morality existed that restrained the people from mistreating one another. And that morality wasn't chased from the public square by the government, because the government logically realized that such morality was playing an essential part in maintaining social order. That's precisely why so many early acts of Congress and state legislatures advanced and encouraged Christian enterprise...not as an effort to force a strict religious code on people, but to promote the moral law.

Yet as morality started to disappear, what

happened? When people began to lose their internal sense of moral restraint, they began taking advantage of each other. They began cutting corners in the market place, abusing their freedoms by committing wicked deeds and harming their fellow man. As this immoral behavior spread, people began crying out to government to protect them by passing laws to prevent the emerging decadence. And the government responded…and responded…and responded, to the point where now our law code is so thick that if we dropped it from the sky, it could demolish small cities.

Now recognize that with every law the government writes, man loses just a little bit more of his freedom. As the state grows – even if it is growing legitimately and at the request of frightened citizens looking for protection – self-government shrinks. As the power of the governing authority expands, the power of the individual contracts. Edmund Burke theorized,

> Men are qualified for civil liberty in exact proportion to their disposition to put moral chains upon their own appetites…Society cannot exist, unless a controlling power upon will and appetite be placed somewhere; and the less of it there is within, the more there must be without. It is ordained in the eternal constitution of things, that men of intemperate minds cannot be free. Their passions forge their fetters.[6]

Follow the connection: as morality disappears, government grows. But as government grows, freedom disappears. It's sort of like saying, "Freedom requires moral law," isn't it, Mr. Hitchens?

So we see it wasn't just Mitt Romney that Hitchens and the secular left were assailing. It was the timeless wisdom of America's founders, and political theorists from Locke to Burke to French philosopher Jean-Jacques Rousseau who articulated the necessity of a moral center in preserving liberty. The latter put it succinctly, "A country cannot subsist well without liberty, nor liberty without virtue."[7]

This is the fatal flaw of modern libertarian thought. While their emphasis on individual liberty is to be admired, and their commitment to strictly limited government is to be desired, the disassociation they demand between government and moral law is unacceptable. While many libertarians recognize the vital nature of virtue in the survival of a free society, they believe that government has no role or responsibility in fostering, nurturing, or promoting that virtue among the masses. They take their "live and let live" philosophy to its logical end, insisting that a person can and must be allowed to freely choose whatever kind of personal morality they desire.

This would work in a perfect world. But in a fallen world, as we've already established in previous chapters, some self-determined visions of morality are not consistent with the Real Morality. A post-modern society, slouching dangerously towards the philosophy of moral relativism, will not willfully embrace the moral law. But Libertarians fatally promote the idea that any morality, any virtue espoused by a society is sufficient. This foolish belief defies logic and denies history. It is not enough to say that government shouldn't care what people do as long as they don't hurt anybody else. As columnist Selwyn Duke explains,

> To paraphrase C.S. Lewis…this is much like having a fleet of ships and saying that you don't care how the vessels function as long as they don't crash into each other. Obviously, if they don't function properly, they may not be able to avoid crashing into each other. So libertarians may say, "Whatever works for you – just don't work it into government," but what about when someone doesn't work properly? Thinking that personal moral disease won't infect the public sphere is like saying, "I don't care what a person does with his health – carry tuberculosis if you want – just don't infect me."[8]

It's why the Founders believed that it was appropriate for the government to take an active role in promoting the moral character of the people, according to the principles of the true moral law. They understood what the libertarians of today conveniently omit: when enough people believe enough immoral things, they will impose that immorality on everyone through the force of law, thus destroying not only morality, but freedom in the process.

Call it the insurmountable obstacle to libertarian thought. Their vision of unfettered liberty is rendered unattainable by their "anything goes" philosophy of personal morality.

Perhaps all of this is illustrated better not in the abstract, but in a real-life scenario. And while virtually any setting would work – the market, the workplace, the home – I prefer one that has a bit more of a scarring impact on me personally: the elementary school playground.

No matter our age, all of us can remember going to recess out on the playground. Whether we played in the days of OSHA-approved plastic jungle gyms, the era of metal slides and monkey bars, or the age of dirt mounds and grassy fields, we all were subjected to the reality of playground rules. Rules like no hogging the jump rope, no pushing, no hitting, no spitting, or no hanging upside down.

Those rules, usually posted on some metal sign in the corner of the playground, were to be followed with no exceptions. So the logical question becomes, what made us follow those rules? Well, I don't know who it was for you. But for me, as a third grader at Rio Grande Elementary School, it was all 6'7 and 450 pounds of the playground monitor standing in the corner of the yard watching us. I was scared to death of that woman…and I wasn't alone.

Every kid on the playground knew that if we broke one of those rules, this beastly woman (who, if I recall correctly, also had about seven different sets of eyes) would grab us by the bottom of the ear and drag us in to see the Vice Principal. No one had ever seen that man and lived to talk about it. He was a mythical figure…the stuff of legends that kept you up at night. And it was that fear, reverence, and respect for the authority of the playground monitor and the Vice Principal that kept us following those rules.

Now, imagine removing the monitor from the playground. What would happen? For a while, everything would most likely continue as it always had

– a common sense of tradition would carry forward for a short period of time. But before too terribly long, someone new to the playground, or perhaps someone who just got a little bold and a little tired of the rules, would decide not to give up the jump rope to the next person in line. And when we pointed to the rules, they would merely scoff and inform us that they made their own rules.

Then someone else, out of anger or spite, would grab a big chunk of little Susie's hair. And many of us would confront them, motioning towards the metal sign and rule #8 that clearly stipulates, "Thou shalt not pull the girls' hair." You can almost hear the response, "Listen you radical, right-wing, Christian, fundamentalist nut…those may be your 'Ten Commandments,' and you may choose to follow them. But I make up my own commandments, my own rules, and you have no right to push your views off on me. Live and let live!"

As that philosophy begins to spread, we find ourselves on a playground in chaos. And as many of us who have experienced what happens when the teacher steps inside or is late arriving to their duty can testify, who always rises to the top of a playground in chaos? The biggest…the strongest…the bully. Everyone becomes subject to the will of the bully until and unless the playground monitor arrives to restore proper order. If she doesn't return, what devolves is not a pleasant picture.

This hard truth is born out in literature as well. In my freshman year of high school I was assigned to read William Golding's well known novel, "Lord of the Flies." Reading through the book, the devolution from order to chaos bears perfect resemblance to our playground analogy.

At the opening of the story, a group of young British boys become stranded on a tropical island when the plane they are being evacuated in is shot down. There, without adult supervision, the boys rely on the traditions they have been exposed to back home, stating in Chapter 2, "We've got to have rules and obey them. After all, we're not savages. We're English, and the English are best at everything."[9]

Just three chapters later, experiencing passions and temptations unbridled by any prevailing sense of authority, the author writes that, "The world, that understandable and lawful world, was slipping away."[10] Indeed it was. By the book's final chapter, the sadistic violence and brutality of life without moral order had caused the book's protagonist Ralph to, "[weep] for the end of innocence, the darkness of man's heart,"[11] and the death of his beloved friend Piggy.

And tragically, this principle is not just theoretical (playground) or fictional (Lord of the Flies). It is also historical. In an effort to liberate himself from any notion of moral authority, man has repeatedly invited the chaos that logically follows. And if history teaches us anything, it is that such chaos is the breeding grounds not for freedom, but for its antithesis – tyranny.

To prove this, simply look at the historical record.

Ivan Karamazov, one of the characters of Russian novelist Fyodor Dostoyevsky's renowned work "The Brothers Karamazov," contended that if there be no God, there exists no moral authority. And without any moral authority, everything is permitted.[12] Certainly this philosophy has been embraced by leading thinkers from French existentialist Jean-Paul Sartre to Danish theologian Søren Kierkegaard, and reached its logical end in the infamous declaration of German atheist Friedrich Nietzsche who boasted, "God is dead...we have killed him...must we not ourselves become gods simply to seem worthy of it?"[13]

Don't look now, but "must we not ourselves become gods" sure sounds a lot like Satan's promise to Eve that "you shall be like God," does it not? Two thousand years, and man's best efforts at arriving at a grand philosophy morally independent of, and superior to that which exists under the sovereign God, have landed him right back in the Garden of Eden. And despite all of his pompous pride, the great mind of humanity remains just as depraved as Eve's.

It is extraordinarily instructive that at the very same time Nietzsche was making funeral arrangements for the Creator God, he was simultaneously predicting that the coming 20th century would be the most murderous in human history. That he was right (compile the gruesome statistics of Hitler, Stalin, Mao, et al on your own time) is actually of secondary importance. Most significant is the apparent recognition Nietzsche had that man, left with no moral authority beyond his own impulses and passions, would devolve into self-destruction.

Indeed the ovens of Auschwitz, the killing fields of Cambodia, and the trash bins of Planned Parenthood bear silent witness to this sad truth: when a belief in God dies, man dies.

Though this conclusion is inescapable, the conceit inherent in humanist thought forbids them from admitting it. Consequently, we are persistently treated to the vapid musings of Nietzsche's modern day prophets like Hitchens and Sam Harris who contend that one must ostensibly choose between religion and reason.

But suggesting that reason alone is sufficient to direct behavior is intellectually dishonest. Human reason will always be guided by presuppositions. That is why civilizations like ancient Rome found it reasonable to murder handicapped children while we in the Western world find that to be abominable.

It was the Roman philosopher Seneca the Younger who explained, "We drown even children who at birth are weakly and abnormal."[14] What would prompt such a barbaric act? Seneca asserted "it is not anger but reason" that provides justification. This horrific practice is the result of reason built upon a Godless foundation.

This reality is why America's Founders chose to establish the philosophical basis of our civilization in something more concrete. It's why they insisted that man's most basic rights were not the gift of his fellow man, or an all-powerful government. After all, if government gave you your rights, government can legitimately take them away. It was Chairman Mao Zedong – whose godless communist regime oversaw the extermination of perhaps more innocents than any other in world history – who expressed that right and wrong is determined by who is standing on the right side of the gun.[15]

Instead, the architects of American government proclaimed that our most basic rights were the endowment of a transcendent moral authority that supersedes man. As a consequence, those naturally endowed rights are inalienable – meaning, man (individually or collectively) has no authority to deprive his fellow man of that which was given to him by the Creator.

But if the source of our inalienable right to liberty is the act of a benevolent God, how wise is it to use that liberty to deny His existence? How long does a tree last when its roots have withered? That is the precise question Thomas Jefferson posed when he first posited, "The God who gave us life gave us liberty,"[16] and then asked,

> Can the liberties of a nation be thought secure
> when we have removed their only firm basis,
> a conviction in the minds of the people that
> these liberties are the gift of God? That they
> are not to be violated but with his wrath?
> Indeed I tremble for my country when I
> reflect that God is just; that his justice cannot
> sleep forever.[17]

This exposes the utter foolishness propagated by those who believe freedom and submission to moral authority are contradictory. Far from being mutually exclusive, they are codependents. Freedom does not – cannot – exist apart from God's moral law.

Dr. Alan Keyes put it this way,

> Freedom requires that at the end of the day,
> we accept the constraint that is required, the
> respect for the laws of nature and nature's
> God that say unequivocally that our
> daughters do not have the right to do what is
> wrong, that our sons do not have the right to
> do what is wrong...The men and women who
> first launched the great experiment in
> liberty...did not [offer]...a vision of licentious
> freedom and stupid self-indulgence. Instead,
> it was a vision of freedom based upon the fear
> of God and the respect for law.[18]

If you struggle to believe that, I challenge you to read George Washington's Farewell Address with an open mind and maintain your skepticism. Of course, as a history and government teacher in the public school system, I advise you not to search for it in your children's textbooks. The Farewell Address has long since been removed to make room for more important things (please note the sarcasm) like the United Nations Declaration of Human Rights.

But once you do find it, you will read words like these:

> Of all the dispositions and habits which lead
> to political prosperity, religion and morality
> are indispensable supports.[19]

Just stop right there and think about that. Here is the Father of the Country saying that the most important elements leading to a happy and healthy society are not free markets and tax cuts...not national defense, foreign trade or sound immigration policy. The two most significant factors in producing a prosperous nation are religion and morality. Washington's sentiments were echoed by fellow founder Abraham Baldwin who concurred, "It should therefore be among the first objects of those who wish well to the national prosperity to encourage and support the principles of religion and morality."[20]

Imagine how an American politician would be treated today if they said something like that, and you see how much ground we have to make up. And we begin by reminding our culture of the wisdom of our Founders. Washington continued, sending a shot right through the heart of the modern secular humanist left:

> In vain would that man claim the tribute of patriotism, who should labor to subvert these great Pillars of human happiness, these firmest props of Men and Citizens.[21]

Did you catch that? Washington is saying that since religion and morality are the vital supports upon which our way of life depends (again, because Christian principle teaches morality, which is the best friend of a free society), it is an unpatriotic act to seek to remove them from the public square.

Yet that is exactly what the humanist left has been pursuing for well over a generation. Because on one hand, the existence of moral authority forbids their pursuit of sexual anarchy, and on the other it demands respecting the autonomy of man over the heavy-handedness of the state, the left vehemently opposes the Judeo-Christian ethic that perpetuates a belief in moral law.

And so beginning largely in the 1960s, the left targeted the American courtroom and schoolroom in an effort to bring about a cultural revolution replacing moral authority with moral relativism. They have established organizations like *Americans United for the Separation of Church and State* and *Freedom from Religion Foundation* who exist for the sole purpose of accomplishing a task that George Washington called un-American. And tragically, they have been remarkably successful.

Through court order and not popular statute, the Christian God has been barred from the classroom, public property, and the halls of government. At the behest of those whose motivation is not respect for all beliefs, but rather bitter hostility to one, the presence of a moral authority is being removed not just from buildings and books, but from the conscience of our people.

Washington went on to warn us what the consequences of such an exercise would be:

> Reason and experience both forbid us to
> expect that national morality can prevail in
> exclusion of religious principle.[22]

Was he right? Has the ill-advised, unpatriotic removal of the Christian heritage of our country resulted in a breakdown of national morality? Has removing the monitor from our society's playground through court cases and textbooks caused us to begin experiencing the chaos and disorder history has demonstrated with frightening regularity?

I turn on my eleven o'clock news and watch in the lead story a bulldozer stick two forks into the lawn of a courthouse, lift two stone tablets, place them on the back of a flatbed truck that disappears off into the distance. The second story of the night warns that a serial rapist has struck again. The third story issues an Amber Alert as another child has been abducted. The fourth story recounts a double homicide on the city's northeast side. And as the litany of bad news continues, my mind cannot help but make the connection between the first story and the ones that followed.

The removal of God from the public square…the removal of a moral authority from our society is not liberating us. It is shackling us. It's not delivering us. It's destroying us. It's not freeing our children. It's forging their chains.

That is why we, the 78, must take seriously our responsibility of leading a revolution of philosophy in our government. One that relies on the wisdom of our Founders to reclaim what we have fatefully let slip away. This doesn't involve establishing a theocracy (we will soon dispatch that hysterical nonsense in the following chapter), or imposing a strict religious code on others.

It means recognizing that at the heart of good government is a primary reliance on, and submission to, moral law. Disregard or disobedience to such authority is culturally devastating and ushers in the collapse of human liberty.

Such is the lesson of history that we are dooming ourselves by repeating. Our playground is in chaos, and the bully will not be long in emerging.

CHAPTER NINE

THE BEST THE WORLD EVER SAW

Suddenly the significance of our "Christian founding" is taking on the proper context. When our Founders spoke fondly of Christianity and Christian principle:

When Benjamin Franklin called it, "the best the world ever saw or is likely to see;"[1]

When James Madison called it "the religion we believe to be of divine origin;"[2]

When John Adams called it "above all religions that ever prevailed or existed in ancient or modern times, the religion of wisdom, of virtue, equity and humanity;"[3]

When his son John Quincy Adams said that "the highest glory of the American Revolution was this: it connected in one indissoluble bond the principles of civil government with the principles of Christianity;"[4]

They didn't say those things because they were rabid extremists and theocrats. They said them because they were lovers of freedom, and they knew that freedom had no greater friend in the world than the precepts and principles established by the Author of human liberty...a title they ascribed to the Creator God of Christianity.

Though not a monolithic group, the architects of our republic shared this common understanding best expressed by John Quincy Adams that, "The laws of nature...of course presupposes the existence of a God, the moral ruler of the universe, and a rule of right and wrong, of just and unjust, binding upon man, preceding all institutions of human society and government."[5] His statement is reflective of the Biblical Christian worldview we encountered in chapters four and five. Our Founders seemed to understand that if so-called "natural rights" like life, liberty and property were not tethered to an immovable, transcendent authority, they would cease to exist.

That's why they didn't leave the concept of natural rights up to subjective interpretation. Key founder James Wilson clarified,

> As promulgated by reason and the moral sense, it has been called natural; as promulgated by the Holy Scriptures, it has been called revealed law. As addressed to men, it has been denominated the law of nature; as addressed to political societies, it has been denominated the law of nations. But it should always be remembered that this law, natural or revealed, made for men or for

nations, flows from the same divine source; it is the law of God.[6]

His contemporary, the brilliant Alexander Hamilton, concurred, stating that the law of nature, "which, being coeval with mankind and dictated by God Himself, is, of course, superior in obligation to any other. It is binding over all the globe, in all countries, and at all times. No human laws are of any validity, if contrary to this."[7]

And where did they turn for the proper articulation of that God-given law upon which all successful manmade laws would be based? Constitutional signatory James McHenry answered, "Public utility pleads most forcibly for the general distribution of the Holy Scriptures...In vain, without the Bible, we increase penal laws and draw entrenchments around our institutions."[8]

McHenry and his fellow Founders understood that without the perpetuation of Biblical morality, adherence to the Natural Law would disintegrate. When that occurred, as we discussed in the previous chapter, an increase in penal laws would be necessary. Such an increase would not yield more liberty, but less. Yet somehow this simple truth evades those who see the preservation of Christian values in our culture as freedom-destroying, when the wisdom of our Founders and the entire history of our civilization teach the exact opposite.

If you need convincing on this point, simply examine this significant portion of an essay written by one of our greatest Founders, Dr. Benjamin Rush. Addressing why he placed such an emphasis on a cultural embrace of Christian principle, Rush persuaded,

> It is not my purpose to hint at the arguments which establish the truth of the Christian revelation. My only business is to declare that all its doctrines and precepts are calculated to promote the happiness of society and the safety and well-being of civil government.[9]

Rush is deliberately rejecting the notion that he (or his fellow Founders) sought to use the power of government to force individuals into accepting the truth of the Gospel message. Evangelism was understood to be the domain of the church, not the government. But notice that did not mean that the government was to be disinterested in the propagation and proliferation of Christian morality. Rush explained why:

> A Christian cannot fail of being a republican...for every precept of the Gospel inculcates those degrees of humility, self-denial, and brotherly kindness which are directly opposed to the pride of monarchy...A Christian cannot fail of being useful to the republic, for his religion teaches him that no man 'liveth to himself.' And lastly a Christian cannot fail of being wholly inoffensive, for his religion teaches him in all things to do to others what he would wish, in like circumstances, they should do to him.[10]

In other words, it was the principles, not the strict doctrinal code flowing from Christianity, that government was to take an interest in promoting. Understanding that the radical, unprecedented experiment in self government they were attempting relied on a pervasive civic virtue among the people, our Founding Fathers thought it wise for government to advance such morality. And given the choice of all the various systems of morality that had existed throughout history, they found the ethics and principles of Christianity to be superior and the most beneficial.

Whether they came to this conclusion because it was their own consciously held belief system (which the evidence undoubtedly demonstrates), doesn't ultimately matter. It's why I won't spend an inordinate amount of pages providing the countless quotations of our Founders that prove their personal allegiance to the Lordship of Christ, nor drone on endlessly about the overwhelming predominance of Christianity in the country at the time of our founding. These are facts that only the willfully ignorant deny, and that are honestly not overly germane to a discussion about the relationship between Christianity and government.

Please know that I am not downplaying the significance of our Founders' personal faith, but simply making the point that they could have been Christians themselves, yet created a governing system that was totally isolated from Christianity. Indeed this is the very argument that many in our culture attempt to make; one that – as we are seeing – is totally untenable.

Though modern day humanists and confused Christians fail to see the distinction, our Founders understood that the government promoting Christian morality is far different than it compelling worship, collecting offerings, and demanding obedience to a strict denominational code. While the latter was unquestionably forbidden, the architects of our republic believed the preservation of our way of life depended upon the former.

It's why George Washington wrote that, "the foundation of our national policy should be laid in private morality,"[11] and again that, "in the progress of morality...to which our Government will give every furtherance, we may confidently expect the advancement of true religion, and the completion of our happiness."[12]

Notice Washington is talking about national laws being based in morality and how government will be furthering morality through its actions. This is not government taking a neutral role in determining whether or not the people will recognize and obey the moral law. And why should it be neutral? It would be like the Pilgrims creating a colony that relied on manual labor, but then not caring if the people became lazy.

Washington's successor, John Adams, confirmed as much when he exhorted that government should be concerned with, "the promotion of that morality and piety without which social happiness can not exist nor the blessings of a free government be enjoyed."[13]

Those in our culture who continue suggesting that it is somehow improper for the government to take an active role in promoting Christian morality not only contradict the explicit words of our Founders, they back themselves into an intellectually embarrassing corner. They must contend that the very men who proclaimed, "Religion and morality...are necessary to good government, good order, and good laws,"[14] and "Christianity [is] necessary to the support of civil society,"[15] created a government incapable of encouraging such. This is abject foolishness.

But what about the First Amendment? Do the words, "Congress shall make no law respecting the establishment of religion, or prohibiting the free exercise thereof"[16] forbid the promotion of moral principle? Not surprisingly, that depends on who you ask.

On the one hand, you have constitutional scholars like Thomas Krannawitter who advise,

> The Establishment Clause of the First Amendment was never intended to prohibit government from advancing religions and morality. On the contrary, the men who framed and ratified the Constitution, as well as the Bill of Rights, believed only a moral people capable of self-restraint can be free, and thus they thought it essential that the government take an active role in promoting the moral character of the American people.[17]

Though this certainly seems to fit with the words of our Founders, it flies in the face of current conventional wisdom. For example, in an unusually high-profile Senate race in Delaware during the hotly contested 2010 midterm elections, Republican candidate Christine O'Donnell was widely ridiculed for the following exchange she had with her Democrat opponent, Chris Coons:

Coons:	The First Amendment ... establishes the separation -- the fact that the federal government shall not establish any religion, and decisional law by the Supreme Court over many, many decades clarifies and enshrines, that there is a separation of church and state that our courts and our laws must respect.
O'Donnell:	So you're telling me that the separation of church and state is found in the First Amendment?[18]

A noticeable murmur of mockery floated through the crowd of students observing the debate at Widener University School of Law. And subsequent media reports pummeled O'Donnell for her ignorant question. I'm still trying to figure out why.

Perhaps it is because later in their exchange, the crosstalk made it appear that O'Donnell questioned the actual words of the First Amendment. But given that the phrase "separation of church and state" does not appear in the First Amendment (or any founding document), the ensuing frenzy provoked by O'Donnell's legitimate question reveals something catastrophic to our culture that we, the 78, must fight to overcome: an entire generation of Americans being raised to believe that the First Amendment says something that it doesn't say.

To illustrate what I mean, look at the press release issued by the left-leaning *American Civil Liberties Union* immediately following an appeals court decision that declared the phrase "under God" in the Pledge of Allegiance unconstitutional when recited in schools:

> Today a federal appeals court in California ruled that the phrase "under God" in the Pledge of Allegiance is an unconstitutional endorsement of religion and cannot be recited in schools...we believe the court's finding was correct.[19]

Examine those words closely. The ACLU celebrates the striking down of "under God" because it amounts to, "an unconstitutional endorsement of religion." Of course, the only way such a conclusion makes sense is if the Constitution forbids endorsing a religion. Does it? No. It forbids an "establishment" of religion.

It could be that the authors of the First Amendment thought that the words "establishment" and "endorsement" should be used interchangeably. Certainly that has become the accepted legal precedent. But if it is not what they meant – if, in fact, they meant what they said – the current misinterpretation of the Establishment clause may be doing untold damage to our culture. It may be being used as a battering ram to obliterate the very Christian principle and morality our Founders sought to perpetuate as the essential pillars of our civilization.

The only way to know for sure is to do something no one seems overly interested in doing: ask the Founders.

Following extensive congressional hearings into the original intent of the Establishment clause nearly sixty years after its ratification, a Senate committee report concluded:

> The [First Amendment] clause speaks of 'an establishment of religion.' What is meant by that expression? It referred, without doubt, to that establishment which existed in the mother-country, and its meaning is to be ascertained by ascertaining what that establishment was. It was the connection, with the state, of a particular religious society,
>
> (1) by its endowment at the public expense, in exclusion of, or in preference to, any other,
>
> (2) by giving to its members exclusive political rights,
>
> (3) and by compelling the attendance of those who rejected its communion upon its worship or religious observances.
>
> These three particulars constituted that union of Church and State of which our ancestors were so justly jealous and against which they so wisely and carefully provided.[20]

Having just emerged from under the shadow of such an unproductive union of church and state, our Founders placed a high premium on the rights of conscience and the ability to worship freely. This had been the tradition of the American colonies beginning

with the Pilgrims. And with such an eclectic array of flourishing Christian denominations, the framers of the First Amendment sought to prevent rivalry and jealousy between those sects.

Their fear that one denomination might independently (or collectively with another) attempt to harness the power of the national government and impose their brand of Christianity as the "Church of America," was the major impetus behind the Establishment clause. James Madison himself recognized this primary concern of the American people when he responded to congressional delegates that he, "...believes that the people feared one sect might obtain a preeminence, or two [Anglican and Congregational] combine and establish a religion to which they would compel others to conform."[21]

If successful, that could have precipitated the same abuses they had experienced under the Church of England's state-run clergy, and that alone is what the First Amendment sought to prevent.

Note then that there is absolutely no pretext to suggest that the intent of the First Amendment was to somehow isolate government from religious principle altogether. This may be the objective of contemporary anti-Christian activists, but it was clearly not the motivation of our Founders. A Senate Judiciary Committee report, investigating this very issue in 1854, affirms that truth:

> They intended, by this Amendment, to prohibit "an establishment of religion" such as the English Church presented, or any thing like it. But they had no fear or jealousy of religion itself, nor did they wish to see us an

irreligious people...they did not intend to
spread over all the public authorities and the
whole public action of the nation the dead
and revolting spectacle of atheistical apathy.[22]

In other words, the last thing the Founders
intended with the First Amendment was to drive
religion from the public square. As we have already
seen, they believed that a free society cannot function
apart from the civic virtue taught best by Christian
principle. Therefore, the idea that they were
attempting to bludgeon that principle from the hearts
and minds of the people is as absurd as it is dangerous.

It is abusing the text of the First Amendment to
conclude that its purpose was to neutralize the spread
of Christian morality in our culture. A House Judiciary
Committee report from that same year of 1854
demonstrated why:

> In this age there can be no substitute for
> Christianity: that, in its general principles, is
> the great conservative element on which we
> must rely for the purity and permanence of
> free institutions. That was the religion of the
> founders of the republic, and they expected it
> to remain the religion of their descendants.
> There is a great and very prevalent error on
> this subject in the opinion that those who
> organized this Government did not legislate
> on religion.[23]

That prevalent error unfortunately persists to
this day. And sadly it has grown to permeate the

minds of the majority of our fellow citizens, including many of the 78. The error has resulted in perhaps well-intentioned, but nonetheless imprudent legal guidelines for testing the constitutionality of laws with a religious component. The so-called Lemon Test, first articulated in the 1971 case *Lemon v. Kurtzman*, being chief among them.

The Lemon Test (along with others it has spawned) is an invaluable weapon for those who seek to obliterate the influence of Christianity in our culture, as it requires every law to pass three requirements:

(1) The law must have a secular purpose.

(2) The law must be neutral towards religion, neither hindering it, nor advancing it.

(3) The law must not result in excessive entanglements between the two realms.

Though popularly regarded as an even-handed approach, the Lemon Test begins with a faulty premise, and thus is fatally flawed. What, after all, is a "secular purpose" anyway? The use of this phrase immediately betrays that its authors presuppose the existence of two different domains: sacred and secular. God may be given domain over the former, but man unquestionably rules the latter.

It's from this unsound starting point that our modern understanding of "separation of church and state" has emerged. I say modern understanding because the concept of separating the institutions of church and state was an ingenious and extraordinarily wise idea of our Founders. There is no question that the church and the state serve two different functions. The church exists to bind believers together and point all men to Christ as Lord. The state exists to facilitate the orderly procedure of man in a fallen world.

These are two distinct roles and they should not be confused. But both of these institutions are gifts of God, and – as the Biblical Christian Worldview teaches – both are under the sovereign authority of God. So while they serve two different functions, both entities are accountable to the Moral Authority for their actions. My preacher and my president have separate jobs to fulfill, but both act under the authority of, and are both answerable to God for the way in which they fulfill them.

This is the proper understanding of separation of church and state – an understanding that we have demonstrated was not lost on the architects of our system of government.

But our modern concept of separation – as expressed here in the Lemon Test – is totally different. God is removed from His sovereign position over all things. He is made the manager of the sacred world, while man is crowned manager of the secular world. Therefore, anything having to do with the church may be answerable to God's authority, but everything else (from government to politics to entertainment to education) is man's domain. Thus, the phrase we should use is not "separation of church and state" at all. It would be much more accurate to term it what it is: *isolation* of church and state. Here's a graphic depiction the difference:

The Founders' understanding of separation:

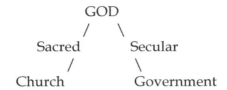

Our modern understanding of separation:

This earth-shattering departure from our foundations is what creates bizarre contradictions between then and now. It's why in early American schools the Bible was the lone textbook, but today it is barred from the classroom. It's why Thomas Jefferson (the supposed architect of the isolation of church and state) held Christian church services in government buildings, but today children are threatened by officials not to mention the name of Jesus at their graduation ceremonies. It's why the same Supreme Court that has the Ten Commandments enshrined above their heads rules those Commandments cannot be celebrated on public land.

It's why during the original debate over the wording of the First Amendment, Representative Benjamin Huntington, expressed concern that, "The words might be taken in such latitude as to be extremely hurtful to the cause of religion." He urged that, "The amendment be made in such a way as to secure the rights of religion, but not to patronize those who professed no religion at all."[24]

How prophetic do those words now appear? In articulating her reckless "Endorsement Test" in 1984, supposedly conservative jurist Sandra Day O'Connor suggested that the First Amendment forbids far more than just a national establishment of religion. She argued that the First also forbid endorsing religion because, "Endorsement sends a message to non-adherents that they are outsiders, not full members of the political community, and an accompanying message to adherents that they are insiders, favored members of the political community."[25]

It is no surprise that O'Connor's foolish precedent was the cited justification in striking down "under God" from the Pledge of Allegiance.[26] What is this if it is not "patronizing those who profess no religion at all?"

Simply apply the actions of our Founders (the architects of the First Amendment) to the tests our modern courts now use to determine what actions violate that First Amendment, and you'll see how demented our current understanding of the relationship between God and government has become.

Would the Continental Congress' purchase of 20,000 Bibles to distribute into the various states[27] pass as having a "secular purpose?"

Would George Washington's command to, "beseech God to pardon our national and other transgressions; to promote the knowledge and practice of the true religion,"[28] pass muster as "neither hindering nor advancing religion?"

Would Congress' 1796 act, "regulating the land given to the Society of United Brethren for 'propagating the gospel among the heathen'"[29] be an "excessive entanglement" between religion and government?

These are questions the secular left does not want to answer. How do I know? I've asked. In an on-air debate with the president of the *Freedom from Religion Foundation,* Annie Laurie Gaylor, I decided to try a bait-and-switch. I took the actions of first president George Washington and attributed them to former Alaska Governor Sarah Palin, and then asked Ms. Gaylor whether those actions were constitutional. Here was our priceless exchange:

> Peter: Can I give you one current day issue with Governor Palin and ask your opinion on it, and then we'll close? Governor Palin is being investigated – some people say this is why she has resigned – for allegedly giving a one thousand dollar land grant, alright, this is government land, to a Christian organization to build an evangelism center. If I made the argument that the values that are taught in that center were consistent with the values and principles necessary for our civilization to endure, therefore it's acceptable, would you agree with me?

> Annie: No.

> Peter: So it's unconstitutional for her to do that?

Annie: Yes.

Peter: Okay, here's my problem. This is my
         problem with your organization. 1795,
         George Washington used a thousand
         dollar land grant to build a church for
         the Oneida Indians.

Annie: (silent pause)

Peter: This, this is where I think there's a
         huge disconnect between the intent of
         the Founders and where we are today.

Annie: (awkward silence)

Peter: It, it's really not Governor Palin,
         maam. It was George Washington.
         Governor Palin doesn't have anything
         to do with it.

Annie: Goodbye! (hangs up phone)[30]

I've been hung up on twice during the course of
a debate on my radio program. And both times it came
as the result of quoting the Founding Fathers. I think
there's something to that. The forces that seek to
uproot our cultural foundations -- and have been
frighteningly successful in their efforts to do so --
realized long ago the reverence and respect Americans
possess for their Founders. And so rather than attempt
the futile task of convincing millions of Americans that
those iconic figures like Washington, Jay, Hamilton and
Adams were wrong in establishing our culture in the
Judeo-Christian ethic, they have spent over a

generation rewriting textbooks and issuing court orders to convince those Americans that cultural foundation never existed in the first place.

It's why law students snicker when a candidate like Christine O'Donnell suggests the left-wing doctrine of separation of church and state is not in the First Amendment. They don't know she's right.

It's why otherwise rational people believe the nonsense that says if you let the Fellowship of Christian Athletes meet on school grounds, then you have to allow the Satanist Club to do the same – it's only fair, after all. They don't even realize that some ideas are obviously better and more productive than others, and therefore can be embraced and endorsed by government even when others aren't.

Our Founders understood that. It's why they said that the Christian ethic was the best the world ever saw. If our culture is to survive, the 78 must usher in a revolution of government where our officials are once again willing to acknowledge and promote the same.

PART FOUR
THE RENEWAL

When we think of eternity, and of the future consequences
of all human conduct, what is there in this life that
should make any man contradict...the laws of religion,
and of God?

— *William Wilberforce*

CHAPTER TEN

SEARCHING FOR LINCOLN

I almost glossed over it. Perhaps it's because the statement was so similar to the frequent excuses offered by other politicians whenever the subject of abortion arises, or perhaps it's because I've grown numb to the mindless chatter of those who speak the language of a "culture of life," but accept cultural practices that breed the exact opposite. Whatever the reason, as I sifted through my radio show prep in August of 2008, I had to do a double take when I came across the transcript of former Virginia governor and Democratic National Committee chairman Tim Kaine's interview on NBC's Sunday morning program, *Meet the Press*.

Talking with host David Gregory about the 2008 presidential campaign, Kaine's shocking performance stands as one of the most incredible demonstrations of our society's deterioration into moral confusion. See if you can catch what I almost missed:

Gregory: When do you believe human rights begin?

Kaine: Well, um, human, human rights broadly, my church teaches, and I do believe that human rights begin early in life at conception or shortly thereafter. And that is my personal belief. But I do not believe the force of the criminal law should compel, uh, others to necessarily follow that to the greatest degree…but you shouldn't be talking about overturning *Roe v. Wade* or criminalizing women and their doctors.[1]

Did you notice what just happened? The chairman of one of the two major political parties in the United States of America just officially condoned the act of murder as morally permissible. When I read through the transcript a second time, it hit me like a ton of bricks: Tim Kaine is not saying that what is conceived in the womb is not human. That is the common line offered by those on the humanist left who seek to justify this morally outrageous act of child sacrifice. They typically suggest that the baby in the womb is nothing but a glob of tissue and cells that is not entitled to any human rights.

But not Tim Kaine. Kaine, a former Jesuit missionary no less, stated his case that he personally believes a child in the womb is a human being and is worthy of human rights. But after establishing that as his view, he astonishingly goes on to say that he doesn't believe we should use the force of law to protect those rights. In other words, "I believe that child is a human being worthy of protection, but I don't think you can use the law to punish those who feel differently."

Pause to consider the sickening reality of such a bewildered position. Imagine me saying: "Sure I believe that you are a human being that is entitled to human rights, but I don't think it's acceptable to use the law to enforce that on others. If someone else sees it differently and wants to kill you, I think it should be okay." If this isn't the very definition of moral and intellectual bankruptcy, those terms have no meaning.

And yet, Kaine wasn't laughed out of the *Meet the Press* studio. Kaine wasn't shamefully driven from his position of leadership in the Democratic Party. Kaine wasn't reprimanded or even called to answer for his unequivocal case for legalizing murder in America.

This has become the deplorable state of our society. The breakdown we have experienced in our churches, facilitated by the backwards leadership of those in government who have ripped our society from its concrete foundations in Moral Authority, has inevitably spilled over into our culture.

It's why in a country that sees 78% of its population claiming the Christian tradition we nevertheless have pornography flooding our streets like open sewers, divorce tearing apart over half of the homes once united in the bonds of holy matrimony, and an epidemic of violent crime that leaves virtually no community untouched.

And it's why on the issue that matters more than any other, men who should – and do – know better, go on national television anyway and make a moral case for murder. There is simply no other topic that better illustrates how degenerate our society has become than our bloodthirsty obsession with killing our children for convenience. Abortion is the great moral dilemma of our day, and finding the courage to obliterate this most offensive display of barbaric selfishness must be the first step in any crusade for cultural renewal.

I always find it interesting when callers to my radio show will challenge me on the importance of abortion in our political dialogue. After proclaiming that it is "settled law," they will lecture me that, "It can't just be about one issue, Peter." Well certainly I care about a great many subjects, but if the issue of basic human rights – the issue of life and death – is not the most important, what is? I've never had anyone come up with an answer to that question.

There's a reason that commentators like Rush Limbaugh have called abortion "our next Civil War,"[2] and why its nearly 40 year legacy casts a deeper and darker shadow than any other sin our people have endured. Though the heinous nature of abortion has no equal in American history, the closest comparison we can draw from our past is the wretched evil of slavery.

The similarities are chilling: then – as now – a large contingent of our population believed themselves entitled to deprive their fellow man of his most basic natural rights. They too considered themselves to be "pro-choice," maintaining that it was a constitutionally protected privilege of theirs to wield the taskmaster's whip over their inferior countrymen.

To justify their immorality, the slave-owning south relied on a tragic Supreme Court ruling in *Dred Scott v. Sanford* that declared slaves to be rightful property of their owners, not viable human beings entitled to protection under the law. As a result, countless Americans suffered brutal and inhuman treatment, even losing their lives.

Today, the pro-abortion movement in our country carries forth the slave-owners' ideology. The plantation masters' whip has been handed off in the form of the abortionists' chainsaw forceps to the modern day prophets of "choice." To justify their immorality, these radical abortion proponents rely on a tragically flawed Supreme Court ruling in *Roe v. Wade* that declared small humans in the womb to be the property of their mothers, not viable human beings entitled to protection under the law. As a result, millions of Americans have been, and continue to be, brutally and inhumanly slaughtered.

The parallels, while astonishing, are not perfect. Consider that though some slaves suffered brutal and vicious treatment, the deaths of the enslaved does not even begin to approach the amount of children that have been massacred. While slaves were deplorably denied their inalienable right to freedom, the aborted have been denied their even more fundamental right to life. And the most concerning distinction between these two horrific chapters of our national story is this: our culture eventually found the moral courage to end the dreadful practice of slavery, but the monstrous evil of abortion continues.

If our civilization is to survive, we – the 78 – must end the killing. We must, as previous generations, find the strength and courage necessary to illuminate the gap between our culture's obsession with convenience and self-gratification and the eternal truths espoused in our Declaration of Independence.

We must end our people's apathy towards evil by forcing it out of the shadows and into the daylight, and exposing the shame it brings upon our generation. We must do our part in making this a more perfect union by demanding a society that doesn't deny, but rather celebrates an unalienable right to life for all men – convenient or not.

Inspired by the Biblical Christian Worldview, we must instruct the minds and awaken the consciences of our people once again to the dignity and worth of every man made in the image of God, reaffirming that uniquely American belief in the value of each individual.

We must refute the dismissive attitude of those who would relegate this topic to being a mere political problem or personal matter, and accurately reveal its fundamental importance. Our society's respect for life determines its destiny, and consequently no other question deserves or demands more attention, from every quarter.

We must therefore passionately and relentlessly press the issue, dismantling the illogical and wicked grounds upon which this culturally debilitating practice is built…so let's get started.

One of the major problems we have in the abortion debate is that we are easily distracted by peripheral issues. We get mired and bogged down talking about emotional and exceptional cases like rape and incest, and consequently lose sight of what should be the starting point of our discussion. As was hauntingly revealed in Tim Kaine's shocking interview, any justification for the act of abortion relies on the idea that the aborted is not human.

If what is conceived in the womb is a human being, any abortion would then be tantamount to murder. Those who argue in favor of abortion rights would be put in the unenviable position of trying to make the case that though it is human, the child's residence in the womb justifies it being killed. In other words, human rights are subjectively dependent upon the location of the human – not exactly a sustainable rationale. This was what made Kaine's defense so appalling. He was acknowledging the humanity of the child in the womb, but then saying he felt like it could be legally murdered. This intellectually bankrupt position is totally untenable – something that even the fiercest defenders of abortion recognize.

During oral arguments in the 1973 landmark case of *Roe v. Wade*, Justice Potter Stewart asked Attorney Sarah Weddington (who was arguing for abortion rights), "If it were established that an unborn fetus is a person, you would have an almost impossible case here, would you not?" Weddington audibly laughed as she was forced to acknowledge, "I would have a very difficult case." Stewart pushed further by positing, "This would be the equivalent to after the child was born…if the mother thought it bothered her health having the child around, she could have it killed. Isn't that correct?" Weddington sheepishly granted, "That's correct."[3]

This shocking and eye-opening exchange is what prompted the author of the seminal *Roe* ruling, Justice Harry Blackmun, to acknowledge that the humanity of the fetus is the crux of the debate. In his majority opinion, Blackmun wrote, "If this suggestion of personhood is established, the appellant's case [for abortion rights], of course, collapses."[4] Blackmun understood that if the Court legally recognized that the unborn child was a human person, they could never give tacit approval for abortion without undermining every law prohibiting murder in the United States.

Yet amazingly, after noting the supreme significance of the question of humanity, Blackmun's majority decided, "We need not resolve the difficult question of when life begins."[5] This inexplicable inconsistency begins to demonstrate why the *Roe* decision is commonly regarded as one of the most vulnerable in the history of the United States Supreme Court, and why after nearly 40 years of precedent it remains ripe for repeal.

Even abortion defenders like Laurence Tribe of Harvard Law School acknowledge that, "One of the most curious things about Roe is that, behind its own verbal smokescreen, the substantive judgment on which it rests is nowhere to be found."[6] What's more, Justice Blackmun's own law clerk, author Edward Lazarus, penned this stinging indictment of the incoherency of the *Roe* decision:

> As a matter of constitutional interpretation and judicial method, *Roe* borders on the indefensible. I say this as someone utterly committed to the right to choose...and as someone who loved *Roe's* author like a grandfather...A constitutional right to privacy broad enough to include abortion has no meaningful foundation in constitutional text, history, or precedent.[7]

Even more damaging to its legitimacy than this, the case for abortion rights has no basis in medical science. After hearing the testimony of some of the world's most well respected doctors, physicians, and medical scientists on the issue of life in the womb, a Senate Subcommittee Report in 1981 concluded,

> Physicians, biologists, and other scientists agree that conception marks the beginning of the life of a human being - a being that is alive and is a member of the human species. There is overwhelming agreement on this point in countless medical, biological, and scientific writings...no witness raised any evidence to refute the biological fact that from the moment of conception there exists a distinct individual being who is alive and is of the human species.[8]

No witness. Biological fact. Think about that. Whether it was Dr. Jerome LeJune of the University of Descartes who confirmed that, "After fertilization has taken place a new human being has come into being. [It] is no longer a matter of taste or opinion...it is plain experimental evidence,"[9] or Professor Micheline Matthews-Roth's testimony that, "It is incorrect to say that biological data cannot be decisive...It is scientifically correct to say that an individual human life begins at conception,"[10] not one of these expert medical minds – regardless of their personal opinions on the issue of abortion – would deny the obvious: what is conceived in the womb is fully living, and fully human.

This awareness must be cultivated in our culture. It is now beyond question that the entire case for legalized abortion is one that totally eschews science, medicine, logic and rational thought. The best justification the abortion movement can offer for the perpetuation of this barbaric practice is a relativistic brand of emotional appeals that offend the intellect and shock the conscience.

For proof, consider what happened at Fort Lewis College in Durango, Colorado, just weeks before the 2010 midterm elections. Debating the two sides of Colorado Amendment 62 (an amendment that would have defined the child in the womb as a person and therefore entitled to legal protection) were spokesmen for Personhood USA and an organization called Advocates for Choice, the college outreach group of the country's largest abortion mill, Planned Parenthood.

After being presented with the biological evidence of the unborn child's humanity, a Planned Parenthood spokeswoman proudly proclaimed to the audience, "We are not going to try to use science or evidence, the fact of the matter is, this is, this is opinion. We all have our own opinions as far as when human life begins."[11]

The utter stupidity inherent in such a statement is hard to digest. Is it seriously the position of Planned Parenthood that what constitutes human life and what does not is merely a matter of personal opinion? A murderer is no longer a murderer if he or she simply declares that they don't believe in the humanity of their victim?

This relativistic tripe makes a mockery of what is legitimately and scientifically known: that the terms "embryo" and "fetus" – just as other terms like "infant" or "adult" – don't refer to nonhumans. They refer to humans at particular stages of development. But this blatant antipathy towards science, expressed by the Advocates for Choice, was just beginning.

Later, that same Planned Parenthood spokeswoman enlightened the audience that, "What is inside a body that cannot function outside its host is not a child."[12] Leaving aside the galling use of the word "host" to define the relationship between a mother and her baby, this argument represents a transparent strategy of misdirection.

Viability – that is, the ability to function independently and autonomously – is an arbitrary line that is drawn to determine what a person can do. It does not determine what a person is. Highlighting that significant detail literally implodes this entire line of faulty logic.

Yet seemingly undeterred by these inconvenient facts, the anti-science activists from Planned Parenthood railed on: "We're talking about science as if it is something that is absolutely concrete, like there is absolute proof that there is life and there is not life."[13] Knowing how to respond to that ridiculousness is difficult, because it demonstrates not only a total disregard of simple biology, but a bizarre contempt for rational thinking. Ignorance is frustrating. But taking pride in ignorance is scary.

And how can we not be frightened when considering that the same Planned Parenthood activists that went on to level further jewels of idiocy like, "science cannot be applied to my body," and "the heart doesn't beat 'til 24 weeks"[14] (medical science has established the heart begins beating at 3 weeks[15]), are the very ones who have crafted our national policy on abortion?

Far from any devotion to the sanctity of science and the Constitution, the humanist left perpetuates this macabre ritual of infant-killing in our culture by trampling legality and rationality, instead appealing to the shifting sands of moral relativism. Nowhere is this more perfectly depicted than in the 1992 Supreme Court case that upheld *Roe v. Wade*, *Planned Parenthood v. Casey*.

Finally given an opportunity to provide some clarity to the muddled mess *Roe* had left in its wake, five justices of the Supreme Court attempted to articulate a more precise justification of the legal and moral grounds for child killing. Their pitiful effort shows that even when given almost 20 years to come up with a better explanation for the gruesome practice, the brightest legal minds can't offer anything beyond a self-defeating quagmire of personal preferences.

They write,

> Some of us as individuals find abortion
> offensive to our most basic principles of
> morality, but that cannot control our decision.
> Our obligation is to define the liberty of all,
> not to mandate our own moral code. At the
> heart of liberty is the right to define one's
> own concept of existence, of meaning, of the
> universe, and of the mystery of human life.[16]

Attempting to fully grasp the breathtaking ignorance of this proclamation is a daunting task. What is the purpose of any law (or any court, for that matter) if it is not to maintain or preserve morality? That's what laws do: declare something to be right and something to be wrong. Imagine consistently applying the Court's logic and saying to the slave, "We find slavery offensive to our most basic principles of morality, but that cannot control our decision." Or, "We find child molesting offensive to our most basic principles of morality, but that cannot control our decision." Such foolishness is to be expected of juvenile minds; it is inexcusable coming from our black robed oligarchs.

Moreover, in their mammoth definition of liberty, the Supreme Court basically endorses societal anarchy by proclaiming that any concept of right or wrong is left up to the individual. This is the bumper sticker mentality: "Don't like abortion? Don't have one."

While this may please those whose consciences have been seared by the corruption of humanist arrogance, it should terrify us that the highest court in the land has been reduced to such drivel. Rather than diligent allegiance to the authority of Moral Law, they have deferred to the wisdom of what they read on the back window of the minivan while parked at a stoplight. Simply apply any other moral issue to this ludicrous ruling and you see the problem: "Don't like slavery? Don't own one." "Don't like theft? Don't steal."

This is the consequence of having a predetermined end that you know violates Moral Law, and yet trying to find any way to justify it. It's why Judge Robert Bork fittingly excoriated the five justices who signed their names to this insanity by writing,

"One would think that grown men and women, purporting to practice an intellectual profession, would themselves choose to die with dignity, right in the courtroom, before writing sentences like those."[17]

It's also why columnist and professor Jeffrey Rosen, the legal affairs editor for the liberal *The New Republic* magazine wrote in 2003,

> Thirty years after *Roe*, the finest constitutional minds in the country still have not been able to produce a constitutional justification…that is substantially more convincing than Justice Harry Blackmun's famously artless opinion itself. As a result, the pro-choice majority asks nominees to swear allegiance to the decision without being able to identify an intelligible principle to support it.[18]

That inability to tie this gruesome practice of child sacrifice to any logical justification compels those who continue supporting it to assume the role of fools. Only by feigning complete obliviousness to the most basic questions can they escape the unspeakable cowardice that defines their refusal to defend the rights of all.

Consider as an example of this weakness the asinine response U.S. President Barack Obama gave to minister Rick Warren during the 2008 presidential campaign. At the Saddleback Civil Forum on the Presidency, Obama and Warren had the following exchange:

> Warren: Now, let's deal with abortion; 40 million abortions since Roe v. Wade. As a

pastor, I have to deal with this all of the time, all of the pain and all of the conflicts. I know this is a very complex issue. Forty million abortions, at what point does a baby get human rights, in your view?

Obama: Well, you know, I think that whether you're looking at it from a theological perspective or a scientific perspective, answering that question with specificity, you know, is above my pay grade.[19]

Simply put, questions that define our respect for human rights cannot be above anyone's pay grade, particularly our leaders. Obama's appalling response shows the dramatic paucity of leadership we are now experiencing. How far we have come from the days of Lincoln. When faced with the great moral question of his day, Lincoln did not equivocate. Instead, he threw down the gauntlet, declaring that,

A house divided against itself cannot stand. I believe this government cannot endure permanently half slave and half free. I do not expect the Union to be dissolved; I do not expect the house to fall; but I do expect that it will cease to be divided. It will become all one thing, or all the other. Either the opponents of slavery will arrest the further spread of it, and place it where the public mind shall rest in the belief that it is in the course of ultimate extinction; or its advocates will push it forward till it shall become alike lawful in all the States, old as well as new, North as well as South.[20]

Had Lincoln deflected the issue of slavery by suggesting it was "above his pay grade," he surely would not hold such an esteemed place of reverence in the collective hearts of his countrymen. Indeed, he would be regarded for what he would have been: a coward.

Further, consider the sickening irony that without Lincoln's fortitude and moral courage, it is highly unlikely we would have seen a man the ethnicity of Barack Obama take the presidential oath of office. Yet when given the opportunity to walk in the heroic footsteps of the Great Emancipator, Obama ran away and hid.

Despite his pretending, Barack Obama is not an ignorant man; he knows the answer to Rick Warren's question. But Obama is also smart enough to recognize that he can't do what Tim Kaine did, acknowledging the child in the womb is entitled to human rights. Because having never in the history of his legislative or executive career supported a measure to protect those rights, he knows the ethical fallout that would follow such an admission. Consequently, he merely answers that way as part of a tactical strategy to avoid answering questions that would expose a wicked devotion to the perpetuation of immorality.

He's not alone. Having thoroughly lost the abortion debate on every ground upon which it is fought – constitutional, legal, ethical, moral, logical – the popular trend within the movement for legalized child killing is to follow Obama's example and play dumb. But this last resort reveals the Achilles Heel of the abortion lobby. By acting confused and pleading ignorance, the secular left commits itself to an unsustainable war of attrition. Eventually, they will be exposed as frauds and the people will come to see through their deceptive front.

That's exactly what occurred in Colorado back in December of 2008. Appearing on radio host Bob Enyart's program, *Bob Enyart Live*, abortion advocate Ilana Goldman was stumped by questions most 2nd graders could answer with ease. Again, this wasn't because Ms. Goldman, the president of Women's Campaign Forum and heralded as one of Washington's "Eight Women to Watch," is ignorant. It is because she has committed herself to defending the indefensible. It is because, like Obama, Goldman quickly realized that even simple statements of commonly accepted biological fact would dismantle her entirely unethical position:

> Enyart: You just said that, "We believe that life begins after birth." I'm sure that's not the case, right? You know that the baby in the womb when he's sucking his thumb, playing with his toes, if they're twins they grab one another, the baby learns his mother's voice as compared to the voice of a nurse or doctor; the baby can actually learn melodies to songs. And let me ask you, is it living? I mean, personhood is one issue, and being alive – like a plant is alive and a rabbit is alive, but a plant is not a

person – so whether you're alive, that's a separate matter from whether something's a person. So do you agree that it's alive?

Goldman: (quiet pause)

Enyart: Just in the biological sense: is it living or is it dead?

Goldman: I'm gonna be perfectly honest, I, uh, I, what you're saying does not make sense to me –

Enyart: I'm asking you if it's living.

Goldman: If you, if you want to talk about what is happ –, what are, what are the realities –

Enyart: I realize you don't want to address the issue of what it is. You'd rather skip over that to talk about strong emotions and majority opinions –

Goldman: I'm not, I'm not skipping over that. I'm really answering your question.

Enyart: Okay, well then could you answer this question? Could you answer this – because you said life begins after birth, I think you overstated your own case – but is it living? Is it living or is it dead? I mean some th – , there's inanimate things like rocks are not living. So the fetus in the womb, it's sucking its thumb, playing with its toes, sleeping, it dreams, is it living? I'm not saying is it a person. Is it living?

Goldman: (quiet pause) I am unwilling to engage –

Enyart: You're afraid of that question.

Goldman: No, I'm not afraid of that question.

Enyart: Well then answer it! Is it living? It's either living or dead.

Goldman: I think, I think, uh, I think the definition of life – what is life, when does life begin, these are questions that people reasonably struggle with.

...

Enyart: Is it alive?

Goldman: I – I want to be perfectly clear.

Enyart: Yeah.

Goldman:	I am not afraid of this question. I just think that it's a ridiculous question.
	…
Enyart:	Okay, before I know what I can do with it, I have to know what it is. Can I dispose of it? Can I throw it out? Can I kill it? Well the question is 'what is it.' And that seems to be – Ilana even though you're a leader on this issue, you seem to be afraid to address that. Let me ask you this: what is a fetus? What is a fetus?
Goldman:	(long uncomfortable pause) What – what's your game here? I, I'm not going to get into larger questions of, of, of –
Enyart:	Of the baby.[21]

When I play the audio of that debate at speaking engagements, the audience is usually laughing hysterically by the end. Though that's understandable given the buffoonery spewed by Ms. Goldman, when you realize that over a million American children die every year because our laws are held hostage by such anti-intellectualism, our astonished laughter should turn to despair.

This barbaric ritual of abortion has been in existence for almost four decades. In our "enlightened" and "sophisticated" era, we have allowed a draconian practice that is on par with the animalistic child sacrifice of ancient times. They sacrificed their children to Molech on the pagan altars; we sacrifice ours to the god of selfishness on the altar of convenience.

This acknowledgement is not merely an indictment of those who tenaciously pursue an expansion of such wickedness, but also those who claim to oppose it. Where is our indignation and righteous anger at the evil that surrounds us?

We can speak of a need for civility in debate, but how much civility must be given to a movement dedicated and devoted to killing children? How much civility needs to be granted to those who take the slave owners' position that one human being has the right to deny another human being their unalienable rights?

Now is a time for choosing. Either what is conceived in the womb is not a human person, or it is. If it's not, then there should be no moral or ethical limits placed upon the practice of abortion. If it is not a human being, it is not worthy of protection or rights, and there is no excuse to infringe upon the autonomy of any woman.

But if it is a human being, then the entire backbone of our civilization, the entire weight of the Moral Law that supersedes every law of man, the very words of our Constitution and Declaration of Independence converge to demand we safeguard the life, liberty, and property of all human persons.

If it is a human being, we must speak forcefully and without hesitation against the evil being done in the false name, "freedom of choice." We paraphrase the words of our forebears like abolitionist William

Lloyd Garrison:

> I am a believer in that portion of the
> Declaration of American Independence in
> which it is set forth, as among self-evident
> truths, 'that all men are created equal; that
> they are endowed by their Creator with
> certain inalienable rights; that among these
> are life, liberty, and the pursuit of happiness.'
> Hence, I am pro-life. Hence, I cannot but
> regard oppression in every form – and most
> of all, that which turns a man into a thing –
> with indignation and abhorrence. Convince
> me that one man may rightfully take the life
> of another, and I will no longer subscribe to
> the Declaration of Independence. Convince
> me that life is not the inalienable birthright of
> every human being, of whatever complexion
> or clime, and I will give that instrument to the
> consuming fire…Numerically, the contest
> may be an unequal one, for the time being;
> but the Author of liberty and the Source of
> justice, the adorable God, is more than
> multitudinous, and he will defend the right.
> My crime is that I will not go with the
> multitude to do evil. My singularity is that
> when I say that freedom is of God and
> abortion is of the devil, I mean just what I say.
> My fanaticism is that I insist on the American
> people abolishing abortion or ceasing to prate
> of the rights of man…[22]

If it is a human being, there can be no
compromises made by which we allow it to be
destroyed – no ultrasound compromise, no waiting
period compromise, no "life of the mother"

compromise (I should stipulate the obvious: if a mother's life is in danger carrying the child to term, the child should be removed from the womb to save the life of the mother. And then every known medical effort should be made to save the life of the child. Save them both. Never does the "life of the mother" demand we actively kill the living child within her.).

If it is a human being, abortion is never justified, and those who argue for it must no longer be treated as though they are on the same plane of moral and intellectual equivalence as the rest of us. They are not. They are advocates of murder.

Abortion is the great moral issue of our day, yet the science, the constitutionality, the morality and the ethics of it were decided long ago. All that remains is for us to have the moral courage to act upon self-evident truth.

Let us be the generation that posterity looks on with fondness as the one that did just that...the one that put an end to the American holocaust...the one that finally turned the page on this most embarrassing and revolting chapter of our history by saying without equivocation:

We stand for God, and therefore we stand for life...and on this issue there will be no compromise.

CHAPTER ELEVEN

Society's Severed Backbone

Nothing prepared me for what I would see that morning when I came down the steps to get ready for school. As I entered the kitchen to get a bowl of cereal, eyes still groggy from sleep, a small yellow post-it note stuck to the coffee pot caught my eye. Though I'm not a coffee drinker, and I was sure the message wasn't meant for me, curiosity compelled me to check it out. And there on the note my Dad had left for my Mom that morning were the words that I have never been able to forget: "Lisa…I find you more stimulating than caffeine."

Yikes. I don't think I can fully express how scarring it is for a 16 year old to read about his Mom stimulating his Dad. I skipped school that day and signed up for psychiatric counseling.

In actuality, notes like that were not overly uncommon in my house. I always saw my parents holding hands, setting aside their personal desires to do things for the other one – or for us kids. My Dad was a busy man, but he always seemed willing to break free from his work just to go with Mom to the grocery store. I know they had fights like any couple does, but we rarely (if ever) witnessed them. And I never heard my Dad speak a harsh word to my Mom…ever. There are so many reasons I look up to and respect my Dad, but none of them more than for the way he loved my Mom. And vice versa.

I was blessed. Because as much as I joke about being scarred by my Dad's provocative love note, I know there are literally millions of heartbroken kids who would give anything to watch their parents actually express affection towards one another rather than vitriol, anger and hostility. There are millions of jaded lives that have been forever marred by the selfish decisions one or both parents made – decisions that broke apart a home and either severed or dramatically altered relationships within that home for good.

This is but one more example of how our humanist pride, seeking "freedom" from the Moral Authority of our Creator, actually shackles us with dire consequences. It should come as no surprise to us that as our cultural elites strut about, instructing us on the need for an open-minded, evolving society, they lead us away from the Biblical idea of family.

As a result, as our society supposedly evolves, the family unit simultaneously devolves. We see that reflected in pop culture. Think of the way society used to view the role of the man in the home compared to the modern caricature of him. We "evolved" from the wise Andy Griffith (*The Andy Griffith Show*) to the bumbling Tim Taylor (*Home Improvement*), from the gentleness of John Walton (*The Walton's*) to the crassness of Al Bundy (*Married...With Children*). But we didn't stop there. Soon even Tim and Al gave way to the idiotic and crude Homer Simpson (*The Simpson's*) and Peter Griffin (*Family Guy*). Is this really the sign of an evolving society? Of course not.

It is the sign of a society that has torn itself free from its moral guideposts – one that has listened to the counsel of fools who assure us that protecting and guarding the institution of family is not necessary. They tell us that clinging to outdated interpretations of family is not conducive to breeding a vibrant society. Instead, we are told to embrace the full gamut of diversity, eschew the antiquated notion of roles in the home, and usher in a brave new world where "it takes a village" to raise a child.

As but one illustration of this recasting of social roles, consider what happened a few years ago at one of this country's most prestigious universities. Lawrence H. Summers was almost run out of his job as President of Harvard for making the fairly obvious observation that men and women are different. Such a declaration was condemned by feminists everywhere as paternalistic and unenlightened. Modern feminism has fermented into a movement that has nothing to do with femininity, but rather one that serves as another convenient vehicle for radically transforming our culture away from the Judeo-Christian ethic.

They and their allies commit themselves to warring against common sense, regarding any suggestion that men and women have different roles in the home as a leftover lie from a chauvinistic age, perpetuated by Bible-banging Neanderthals. They are the ones on the front lines to create gender-neutral clothing and textbooks. They demand the integration of high school sports teams, suggesting that differentiating between girls and boys is offensive. Actually, what's offensive is to think about my little girl being closely guarded by a hormone-driven high school boy on the basketball court.

But oblivious to common sense, these cultural reformers lobby everyone from legislators to Hallmark to rid our culture of "Mother's Day" and "Father's Day," as well as "Boy Scouts" and "Girl Scouts" in order to achieve their egalitarian designs. And yes, they are the ones who are so committed to their cause that they find unisex, open bathroom facilities preferable.

That's always interesting to me, given that bathrooms are a great place to notice the obvious differences between men and women. No, I'm not making a crude reference to our biological differences. That seemingly obvious distinction seems lost on these geniuses anyway. But have you ever noticed the difference between men and women using public restrooms?

Men walk in by themselves, keeping their heads up and eyes straight forward as they stand at the urinal. When possible, a buffer urinal is left empty between them. Conversation, if any, is to be brief, general, and to the point. No elaboration, no hanging around, no fluff.

Women on the other hand, visit in packs. They exchange lip gloss and make-up, carrying on extended conversations throughout their experience. Many times women will come out of the bathroom having made a new friend. By contrast, men who go to restrooms to make friends are the kind that you avoid at all costs.

Obviously I'm making light of all this, but the truth is that we refer to our counterparts as the "opposite sex" for a reason. And the reason is that we're different. It is the eternal struggle for men to figure out what a woman is thinking. And for women, it is the eternal annoyance to try to figure out why a man thinks the way he does. Failing to accept that reality, or pretending for the sake of some humanistic political agenda that those differences don't exist, absolutely cripples relationships...including the one providing the foundation of family: the man/woman marriage.

I remember watching my Mom and Dad and marveling at how different they were. Dad was so intellectual and always had a complicated way of approaching everything. Even when he was telling me to be quiet, he found the most complex way of saying it. I remember once he came to the steps to tell me to keep it down. But instead of just saying that, he called out, "Son, this is not a gymnasium or a riot convention. So please desist from excessive decibel emanation."

On another occasion he was scratching his head for a lengthy period of time. Rather than just explaining, "Man, my head itches," he instructed us that, "Apparently the niacin in my scalp is causing the capillaries in my hair follicles to dilate."

Mom wasn't like that. At all. She was much more impulsive, direct, and easy to read. If she was upset, you knew it. And at the same time, if you were looking for compassion she would offer it immediately rather than a thirty minute lecture on the purpose of human suffering.

They were so incredibly different in their approach. And what made them such effective parents was that they didn't try to change the other one to be like them. There were times Dad's analytical approach desperately needed to be balanced by Mom's empathy. And there were times when Mom's emotional approach desperately needed to be countered by Dad's thoughtful logic. I will forever be grateful that Mom and Dad both realized that the differences in their spouse were more about preference and style than they were about some personality flaw that needed to be corrected.

And I know where they learned that principle. God's Word teaches us that He intended the different sexes to play different roles in the home. And in order to fulfill those roles, He naturally gifted men and women differently. He knew Moms would be the backbone of the family, raising the children and being their outlet and sounding board. And so He gifted them with an empathy and sympathy that most men just don't have.

Conversely, He intended Dads to be the decision makers in the home, providing moral clarity and leadership in the midst of struggle. And so he gifted them with a logic and reasoned sense of judgment that most women lack.

Obviously there are circumstances where that isn't the case. My wife Jenny always tells me that between the two of us, I'm more emotional…and it makes me cry every time she says that. Okay, not really. But there are exceptions to every rule. There are also unfortunate circumstances that occur preventing one parent from being present in the home, whether that's death, divorce or other extenuating obligations.

None of this is meant to suggest that raising a child Biblically demands we all follow this recipe perfectly, or that those for whom these guidelines become impossible are destined to fail as a parent. It simply means that this model is what we should strive for, what we should embrace, and what we should promote. Because when it is employed, it works best for children, adults, and society at large. Study after study – from Christian and non-Christian researchers alike – demonstrate that the best predictor of a successful and well adjusted child is an intact nuclear family. Yet, in what amounts to another demonstration of our outright rebellion to Moral Authority, our society unwisely celebrates and encourages disastrous alternatives.

We attack the Biblical model of family as though it is somehow stunting our progress as a people. We confuse the roles and responsibilities in the home, thereby embittering spouses against one another and breeding the most nefarious threat to stable marriages: selfishness.

By eliminating the Divine from the equation of marriage, it becomes nothing but a linear contract with obligations for each spouse to fulfill. And just like any other contract where one party doesn't seem to be living up to their end of the bargain, our first reaction is to take them to court and seek restitution and breech of the contract. The advent of no-fault divorce makes this routine business in America. I can just check the box of "irreconcilable differences," and I'm free from any obligation or expectation of effort. And don't worry about my kids. They're resilient and will get over it. What matters most is that I'm happy.

Though the Biblical model tells us that the point of marriage is for the "two to become one flesh,"[1] we arrogantly embed the exact opposite into our consciences: marriage is about having my needs met; and if they're not, I deserve better.

Indeed, the majority of affairs are born out of this selfish vision. The mistress makes the man feel wanted and respected. The other man makes the wife feel desired and attractive. By isolating ourselves from the covenant concept of marriage, where our obligation to love and sacrifice for our spouse are our primary responsibility to God, we invite a deadly mindset that is devastating marriages and our culture.

After decades of celebrating divorce, what have we found? We've found that divorce, despite its luring promise to eliminate the stress of a struggling marriage, only attracts more potent stressors: divided families, child discipline issues, individual strife, unresolved conflict, personal doubt, a nagging sense of failure, and embittered relationships. It's no surprise then that research indicates divorce does not reduce the symptoms of depression, does not improve self esteem, and does not raise any of the twelve measures of psychological well being.[2]

I remember flipping through the channels and stopping on MTV when I saw fading pop starlet Britney Spears, having just gone through a second dissolved marriage by age 25, talking with teenagers about love. I can't recall her exact words when asked by an audience member how you know you're in love enough to be married, but it went something like this: "Love is all these mixed up feelings. If you're not careful, things can get out of control and soon you might not be in love anymore."

I contrast those words with the ones spoken to me and my wife (then fiancé) by a member of our church congregation who came to our wedding shower. All of the ladies had gathered in a circle and were each giving one piece of advice on how to have a successful and long-lasting marriage. When it came to be Rebecca Ellis's turn, you could see her frail, 90 year old mind attempting to come up with something profound. Finally she looked up and said, "All I can say is just fight through it." By our society's standards, that wasn't the most romantic thing to say. But Rebecca and Bob were married for 70 years. I think she's earned the right to be heard.

And her testimony again confirms that our culture's best attempts to free itself from the expectations of a Moral Authority only results in more pain, more hardship, more despair. Marriage isn't about feelings and shallow romantic lusts. It's about a commitment of the will, and should be regarded as something worth fighting for at any cost.

But beyond those internal temptations that threaten to break down the man/woman family from within, come equally menacing external dangers. That we live in an over-sexualized culture is patently obvious. A simple trip through the grocery store check out line is to encounter magazine covers loaded with sexual imagery and lust-inducing headlines. Doing a simple web search for the most mundane stories or objects is to invite an inadvertent pop-up ad or accidental mis-click directing your browser to a site full of blatant pornography. Even confining your movie-going to strictly PG films does not protect you from scantily clad actors or actresses and overly suggestive humor.

In preparation for a speech on pornography in our culture, I did an experiment that I challenged the audience to try as well. For five straight nights, I turned on my television to each of the network channels (ABC, CBS, NBC, and FOX) sometime during the primetime hours of 8-10 pm. With a stopwatch in hand, I recorded the seconds – yes, seconds – it took on each channel before hearing or seeing something sexual in nature. Whether it was during a commercial break, a sitcom, or a TV drama, for the full week I never went more than 15 seconds on any channel before hitting "stop." Obviously this was not a scientific study. Maybe it was pure coincidence, maybe it was just one of those weeks, maybe my definition of "sexual in nature" was different than what others would apply…or maybe not. Maybe this speaks to how depraved we have become as a culture.

Remember again that 78% of Americans claim the Christian tradition. If 78% of the population was following the Biblical precept to dwell only on what was true, noble, right, pure, lovely and admirable,[3] would Hollywood find the profit margins they need to keep peddling smut? Would magazine companies find it lucrative to put less than half-dressed women on their covers? That they do is an indictment on those of us who have been instructed to, "not conform to the pattern of this world,"[4] but transform our minds and hearts to the Biblical command of self-control.

If there was ever an ideal foreign to our culture today, it's self-control. Beginning in the middle of the 1900s, that concept became an outdated and prudish relic as the sexual revolution took hold in American society. Prompted by the landmark works of zoologist Alfred Kinsey, Americans began shifting their attitudes about sexual behavior. Secretly and deceptively using some of the most degenerate people in the country as his samples (prisoners, ex-cons, child molesters, prostitutes, those who practiced homosexuality and bestiality), Kinsey fraudulently produced data he claimed was representative of average citizens. That data, revealed in his books *Sexual Behavior in the Human Male* and *Sexual Behavior in the Human Female*, purported that most Americans were freely engaging in conduct that at the time was considered depraved: homosexuality, adultery, pre-marital sex, self-gratification. Kinsey and his acolytes then used these statistics to urge what they saw as a straitlaced culture to shed its fear and shame, and begin embracing "free love."

It is most ironic that this Kinsey-birthed movement that grew into the flower-power hippies and currently manifests itself in the modern homosexual agenda is known as "free love," given that its consequences are so shackling and debilitating. Consider what we know of pornography. Besides being a now multi-billion dollar industry, what are the effects it provokes?

Author Norman Cousins conveys the personal dangers of this restless evil:

> The trouble with pornography is not that it
> corrupts, but that it desensitizes; not that it
> unleashes the passion, but that it cripples the
> emotions; not that it encourages a mature
> attitude, but that it is a perversion to infantile
> obsessions; not that it removes the blinders,
> but that it distorts the view. What we have is
> not liberation, but dehumanization.[5]

In other words, while pop culture has us believe
that pornographic images feed our sexual appetite and
can even improve our marital sex lives, the exact
opposite is true. What they feed is a discontent with
our spouse that transforms our understanding of sex
into nothing but a lust-filled release of pent up sexual
aggression. Seeing the potential danger in such a
warped view of what was intended by God to be the
loving and private act of two married individuals
pleasurably meeting each others' physical needs is not
difficult.

Dr. Mary Anne Layden, the co-director of the
Sexual Trauma and Psychopathology Program at the
University of Pennsylvania's Center for Cognitive
Therapy, testified before Congress in 2004 that
pornography is, "the most concerning thing to
psychological health that I know of existing today."[6]
Contradicting the Hollywood wisdom, she confirmed
that porn viewers, "spend so much time in unnatural
sexual experiences with paper, celluloid and
cyberspace, they seem to find it difficult to have sex
with a real human being...Pornography has raised their
expectation and demand for types and amounts of
sexual experiences at the same time it is reducing their

ability to have sex."[7]

In other words, pornography doesn't help your sex life...it kills it. And why wouldn't it? Compare it to eating junk food all day. Is there any better way to spoil your actual meal than to snack on Oreos, Fritos and Ding Dongs? Is it any wonder that divorce lawyers continue to rank accessed online pornography as one of the leading causes of dissolved marriages in the country? After all, pornography is always a conscious choice. It certainly can become fueled by addiction, but when we turn to pornography, we are sending the message to our spouse, "You are inadequate."

This is why a male friend of mine has adopted a zero tolerance policy on any form of pornography. When he and his wife go to the movies and a woman appears on the screen in little clothing, he will turn and just look at his wife. Now, you know that every other guy in the theater is saying to himself, "How whipped is that guy?!" But my friend doesn't care. He's doing it because he's trying to send a conscious message to his wife that she is not in competition with anybody – not even those actresses on the screen.

It's a good example to follow. After all, the marital vows include the words, "forsaking all others." That should mean all others – even those in movies, in magazines, walking past us in the mall and laying on the beach.

Some will argue that pornography is simply harmless adult entertainment. They ignore the concerning reality that an addiction to porn rarely stays confined to looking at pictures. Like any addiction, it breeds experimentation. Repeated exposure to the

Sports Illustrated Swimsuit Edition will eventually cause the viewer to need more stimulation. Having tired of such soft-core pornography, they desire something more graphic. But eventually that too gives way to something else like aggressive or violent pornography. From that point, the now fully depraved mind begins seeking the increasingly bizarre, whether that be homosexuality, bestiality, or other manifestations whose consequences can be disastrous.

Consider the words spoken to Dr. James Dobson by notorious serial killer Ted Bundy shortly before his execution for the violent rapes and murders of multiple women:

> Like other kinds of addiction I would keep looking for more potent, more explicit, more graphic kinds of material. Like an addiction, you keep craving something that is harder, harder, something that gives you a greater sense of excitement. Until you reach the point where pornography only goes so far. You reach that jumping off point where you begin to wonder if maybe actually doing it will give you that which is beyond just reading about it and looking at it.
>
> ...
>
> Listen, I'm no social scientist and I haven't done a survey. I don't pretend to know what John Q. Citizen thinks about this. But I've lived in prison for a long time now and I've met a lot of men who were motivated to commit violence just like me. And without exception, every one of them was deeply

involved in pornography; without question,
without exception, deeply influenced and
consumed by an addiction to pornography.
There's no question about it – the FBI's own
study on serial homicide shows that the most
common interest among serial killers is
pornography.[8]

Reading these words and then considering that
the same organization (the ACLU) that dedicates itself
to preventing children from praying in the name of
Jesus at graduation ceremonies, legally defends access
to pornography as a constitutional right, demonstrates
the challenge before us.

Kinsey's promise that shedding traditional,
Biblical standards would result in a freer, happier
society has proven as empty as all others conceived
apart from Moral Authority. We have found that
tearing down the protective sexual barriers established
by God in order to feed our carnal appetites has
unleashed a barrage of unintended consequences that
we are now powerless to stop.

As one depraved obsession leads to another new
experimentation, we continue hurdling down a dark
path, watching helplessly as our culture begins to take
on a frightening resemblance not to any manmade
utopia, but to Sodom and Gomorrah.

DAYS OF DEPRAVITY

It was a banner week on my radio show. On Monday, I covered a local story about the emergence of an undercover group of "swingers" – a collection of promiscuous married folks who partied together and would regularly swap partners for a night. On Tuesday, I discussed the tragic death of a young man caught up in homosexuality. He had been victimized by two adult men who killed him in the course of fulfilling their violently grotesque fantasies. Wednesday brought a debate on teenage pregnancy; Thursday I lamented the opening of a local strip club; and on Friday, we rounded things out with a denunciation of premarital cohabitation.

Had I known the stories were going to unfold that way, I could have billed it as "Depravity Days on the Peter Heck Radio Show." But what stuck with me more than the litany of stories regarding these dangerous sexual practices was the angry response I received from a handful of listeners after each day. Look at just three of the emails and see if you don't notice something similar about each of their objections.

Here was a response I got to my "swingers" condemnation:

> If you're comfortable confining yourself to one person in marriage, great. But other people may find fulfillment in doing things differently. Who says your way is right? If both partners are okay with it, you shouldn't have anything to say about it.

Strikingly similar was the reaction I got to the homosexuality story:

> Nice to see you trying to use a tragedy to score political points, Heck. In case you didn't know, there are a lot of perverted and dangerous heterosexuals too. You're just using this as one more excuse to try to tell people they have to have the kind of sex you think is appropriate.

And then with eerie parallels to the first two came a defensive strip club patron:

> It's a free country. Maybe you should quit being such a prude. Some women like to go to strip clubs too. If you and your churchy friends don't like it, here's an idea. Go pray or something instead and leave people alone.

Regardless of which erotic practice they were defending – consensual adultery, homosexuality or

CHAPTER TWELVE

"adult entertainment" – the justification was the same: "We can do what we want to do and just because you don't like it, you have no business telling us it's wrong." I think it was at that point that the puzzle pieces fell into place for me: the revolution Kinsey instigated was not just a movement leading to *Playboy* and *Hustler*. He instituted a movement for sexual anarchy, by giving organization and validation to the unrestrained passions of human nature. Due to its utter rejection of Moral Authority, this movement quickly found a home in the secular left's agenda.

It comes as no surprise then that in the years since he died, researchers such as Dr. Judith Reisman have exposed how much of a disgraceful pervert Kinsey was himself. Not only did he intentionally and unethically taint his samples to produce the results he wanted – results that matched his own depraved lusts – we now know that Kinsey was involved in some diabolical sexual experimentation on children as young as 2 months old that amounts to institutional pedophilia.

In just one heartbreaking story, a woman now in her 70s and going by the pseudonym of Esther White has come forward with evidence and testimony that Kinsey paid her grandfather and father to sexually molest her beginning when she was just 7 years old. She recounts:

> In 1943, when I was nine, I found a sheet of paper that had boxes on it and my father was checking off things he was doing to me. He grabbed it away from me and put it in a brown envelope. It was a form with little boxes down the left side of the page, and a list

> of statements describing sexual acts. He was
> supposed to check things off, whether he did
> that or not. One of the statements included
> the words 'timed orgasms.' I didn't know
> what 'orgasm' meant, so I asked him and he
> told me. That's why he was using a
> stopwatch. My dad took movies of what he
> did to me. They were home movies, the
> camera was one of those wind-up types...I
> think he sent them to Kinsey.[1]

This account is but one sick example of the man adored and venerated amongst left-wing academics and cultural elites who continue to perpetuate the myths of Kinsey's breathtakingly corrupt scandal. To their eternal shame, Indiana University still houses and operates the Kinsey Institute, utilizing taxpayer dollars to keep the sexual revolution alive and well.

And from this basis of fraud has come the unrelenting march towards sexual anarchy: school condom distribution, sex education curriculum for children as young as kindergarten, a Hugh Hefner inspired culture awash in pornographic images, and now the movement's current manifestation in the homosexuality and transgendered crusade. Tragically, those of us who seek to oppose these things so often fail to acknowledge they are all tied together. We attempt to fight them piecemeal without slaying the underlying dragon that breathes life into each.

As writer Robert Knight explains, "Millions have been hurt by the false view of sexuality hatched in criminal fashion by Alfred Kinsey and his associates. If Esther's story and that of other victims is widely known, the Kinsey castle would come crashing down, bringing with it a sex education establishment dedicated to raping children's innocence, plying them with condoms and pushing them toward either the abortion clinic or a gay bar."[2]

In other words, these threats to the family all flow from the same foundation. And those of us attempting to bring about a cultural renewal must not only recognize this, but commit ourselves to dismantling that foundation – the quicker, the better. Yet, the major problem we continue to face in doing so is that many of us have now been raised in the Kinsey culture and therefore speak its language.

This is incredibly dangerous given that the words we use can dramatically alter the landscape of our debates over this ongoing sexual revolution and often limit our effectiveness in combating its assault on the family.

Consider the current expression of the sexual anarchy movement. The homosexual agenda has experienced extraordinary growth and success in recent decades. But how does such a repulsive violation of the Moral Law like homosexuality gain growing acceptance in a culture founded on the premise of obedience to that Law? Besides the self-evident tactics of propaganda and a relentless normalization campaign waged by these sexual revolutionaries, our politically correct language has caused us to cede the moral high ground in this struggle.

A majority of Americans (even many within the church) have come to believe in the existence of a group of people whose natural state is "homosexual." We now casually use this terminology, assuming that there are "heterosexuals" and "homosexuals." But when we accept this baseline, we have detached ourselves from rational thinking.

Speaking to a convention of high school students on the topic of homosexuality, I asked someone in the crowd to define for me what a homosexual was. I had a few hands go up, and I chose a young man to answer. He stood up and said, "Someone who has sex with a person of the same sex." I asked him if experimenting with it just once was enough to be termed a homosexual forever, or if a person had to repeatedly engage in that act. He wasn't sure, but eventually decided that once probably wasn't enough.

Others disagreed. I had another young lady stand up and say that if you have a homosexual encounter once, you are a homosexual for life. I asked her, "So if a college girl has a sexual encounter with her roommate, but then goes on to marry a man, have a family, and never again engages in that activity of homosexuality, she is a lesbian no matter what she says?" The girl shrugged and sat down.

I asked them about a singer from the 1990s named Sinead O'Connor. She proudly called herself a lesbian, but then later decided to marry a man. What is she? What about a man who was never interested in homosexuality until he went to prison and found it his only option? Is he a homosexual? What about the person who has urges to engage in homosexuality but never acts on them? Do you have to engage in the activity to be a homosexual or is just fantasizing about it enough? Or what about the woman who leaves her husband of 20 years for a female lover? Does she count, or does she have to be with that lover for at least 20 years before it outweighs her "heterosexuality?"

It didn't take long before they understood the point: there is simply no way to define someone as a homosexual. Why? Researchers compiling the book *Sex in America: A Definitive Survey* put it this way: "People often change their sexual behavior during their lifetimes, making it impossible to state that a particular set of behaviors defines a person as gay."[3]

So why is this a big deal? Why does it matter? Because when we accept the idea that there is some group of people identified as "homosexuals" and another as "heterosexuals," we have allowed the debates over open homosexuality in the military, marriage rights, hospital visitation and other legislative objectives like adoption privileges to become ones of civil rights and fairness. And once those advancing homosexuality have successfully framed these debates in this way, those of us holding to traditional morality are helpless. We are easily portrayed as cruel, discriminatory, hateful bigots unwilling to extend the rights we claim for ourselves to others who are not like us. Needless to say, this is all by design. It has been the stated strategy of the sexual anarchists from the start.

Yet all it would take to undo this fraudulent charade is the basic common sense that all sexual behavior – married heterosexual conduct, adulterous heterosexuality, bestiality, necrophilia, homosexuality, pedophilia, coprophilia, polyamory...ALL of it – is chosen behavior. No one is compelled into any sexual conduct. Even those who choose to abide by God's design for sex within the confines of a married, monogamous, man/woman relationship, how, when and if they engage in sexual behavior, is a choice.

I could wake up tomorrow and proclaim that I was going to abstain from sexual conduct for the rest of my life. And then I could follow through (though it probably wouldn't go over well at home), because regardless of any urge, temptation, lust or desire, sexual behavior is either chosen or not chosen. It has nothing to do with unalterable, unchangeable, immutable characteristics.

A person's natural state is that of male or female. From there, people choose what kind of sexual behavior, if any, to participate in. They choose whether to conform to biblical standards, societal standards, or no standards at all. But since what they do sexually is always chosen behavior, it has nothing to do with their identity. Who a person is, is different than what a person does.

Once we regain this rational baseline for our thinking, we soon realize how terribly and intentionally skewed our cultural perception of the homosexual and transgendered agenda (which is the current manifestation of the push for sexual anarchy) has become.

The recent furor over the repeal of the U.S. military's "Don't Ask, Don't Tell" policy is a perfect example. The ban that had existed from the infancy of the American military until recently was not on any group of people...it was on the open practice of a chosen sexual behavior. Moreover, homosexuality was but one of many sexual practices that had been banned by the Uniform Code of Military Justice. Even attempts of heterosexual adultery are forbidden.[4] (Perhaps we should consider that discriminatory against heterosexuals?)

Therefore, the proper debate regarding "Don't Ask, Don't Tell" should not have been regarded as one determining whether certain people could serve. That is a false premise. The debate should have been held over whether or not those who do serve should be banned from participating in certain sexual behaviors.

Since the Uniform Code of Military Justice seeks, "to promote the well-being, morale...and good order and discipline" of our armed forces, we should be asking whether the open practice of men having sex with men is dangerous to military cohesion. We should be asking whether or not the devastating physical effects of men having sex with men are conducive to a healthy and strong fighting force. We should be asking if the preponderance of sexual transmitted diseases found in men having sex with men represents any concerns with the necessity of battlefield blood transfusions. We should be asking if the same reasons the military forbids men and women from sharing barracks (avoiding sexual aggression, harassment and counterproductive distractions) should not preclude the open acceptance of men having sex with men.

Instead we're plagued with inflammatory accusations of bigotry, based on the very fraudulent grounds that were the hallmark of the father of this sexual revolution, Alfred Kinsey.

Moreover, consider these revolutionaries' assault on marriage. There again, just like our reckless use of "homosexual" and "heterosexual," those of us fighting to defend man/woman marriage as the linchpin to society's most important institution do ourselves immense damage by publicly stating our opposition to the "redefinition of family." That's not what the advocates of same-sex marriage are after. It can't be, given that the activists have offered up no replacement definition for the institution's traditional understanding.

Actually, they can't offer one. Because the moment sexual anarchists define marriage (in other words, place parameters for what constitutes marriage and what does not), they would be guilty of the very act of moral exclusion they condemn in others.

For instance, if they seek to redefine marriage to mean the union of two human beings (regardless of gender), they have excluded from their definition those whose preferred sexual expression is polyamory or polygamy. At that point, the very arguments they have leveled against proponents of "traditional marriage" get turned around on them. They become the bigots, the haters, and the narrow-minded, seeking to deny rights to others just because they're different.

Therefore, you will not hear them offering any new definition for marriage. Their objective is to simply "un-define" it, rendering the institution meaningless and open to any interpretation, any manifestation of what someone considers personally pleasurable. That is precisely why pro-polygamy groups like Polygamy Day, Inc. celebrate each court victory experienced by the homosexuality activists. The polygamists understand that once marriage is undefined, there is no barrier left to hinder their cause either.

As evidence of this, consider a recent story that appeared in the *Salt Lake Tribune*. Columnist Lindsay

Whitehurst reported that the nearly 38,000 polygamists in Utah were closely following a case in Canada where a court was weighing a decision that would upend the country's ban on polygamy. What was astounding about the story was how frighteningly similar the polygamists' arguments were to those we are currently hearing from the homosexual and transgendered crowd in America.

Calling the proceedings "historic," polygamy advocate Marlyne Hammon proclaimed, "If Canada were to drop that law, it would send quite an important message out to the world. They can see [polygamy] is not what everyone says. It's about people."[5] Hammon added that the decriminalization of plural marriage in Canada would be a huge motivation to those fighting for its legalization in America. "We've established ourselves in our homes," she said. "We want to continue fighting for our civil rights."[6]

Utah's Attorney General's office spokesman Paul Murphy said of the case, "I think it will inform us. Canada is tackling the same issues we have, in that we have this law but for the most part it hasn't been enforced by any law enforcement agency."[7]

Notice the similarity in language and sentiment being utilized: civil rights, anti-discrimination, self-fulfillment, personal happiness, don't judge, constitutional rights, personal expression. The very catch phrases currently employed by the sexual anarchists to achieve the acceptance of homosexual behavior are already being used to advocate for the next rung in their ladder.

Once the trail has been forged by homosexuality activists, polygamy is nothing but the next logical step.

Paul McCormack, a law professor at the University of Utah, confirms that if the Supreme Court takes up the question of same-sex marriage, it will open the door to other forms of personal sexual preference. "That would resuscitate the interest in polygamy,"[8] he stated.

In light of all this, I simply ask those who support the legalization of "gay marriage" how they plan to deny marriage rights to those who advocate for polygamy? This has now gone beyond a slippery slope hypothetical question and has entered the realm of reality. The question deserves an answer, and any sane culture would demand one before proceeding further down the Kinsey path.

If we remove the current moral guideposts defining marriage as the God-intended union of a man and woman, declaring them to be a violation of the civil rights of those who want to engage in homosexuality, how do we reposition those posts to reject the civil rights claims of polygamists?

If we accept the arguments espoused by pop culture homosexual activists like Ellen DeGeneres who plead, "People are gonna be who they're gonna be, and we need to learn to love them for who they are and let them love who they want to love,"[9] how do we rebuff polygamy activists like Marlyne Hammon who say the same?

The answer is we don't. That is the consequence of "un-defining" marriage -- it becomes a meaningless term, once for all vanquished by the forces of sexual anarchy. This necessarily opens the floodgates to the legalization of every form of sexual activity, from polygamy to incest to bestiality.

The grave danger this represents should be apparent. Un-defining the nucleus of the family is tantamount to saying that the family is insignificant and unimportant in the preservation of society. But reason and experience both tell us otherwise. Thus, opposition to same sex marriage is not motivated by a fear of some imminent onslaught of homosexual warlords, as the media caricature of our cause depicts. Rather, it is born out of a keen understanding that the voices advocating it are part of a larger movement seeking to radically transform our culture.

Paula Ettlebrick, once the policy director for the National Center for Lesbian Rights, confirmed as much, stating, "Being queer is more than setting up house, sleeping with a person of the same gender, and seeking state approval for doing so...Being queer means pushing the parameters of sex, sexuality, and family; and in the process, transforming the very fabric of society."[10]

Ms. Ettlebrick and her cohorts are foot soldiers in the Kinsey revolution, and they know the success of their cause depends upon the total abolishment of the Judeo-Christian ethic and the Moral Authority it teaches. That is why any belief that the homosexual lobby is merely a passive group of individuals wanting to peacefully coexist with others who have different beliefs and values is naively absurd.

To prove this point, I asked homosexual activist attorney Andrea Ritchie in an on-air debate on my radio show whether, in her estimation, the demands being made by the homosexual lobby could legally coincide in our society with the preservation of traditional, Biblical morality. After stating her opinion that there is no homosexual or transgender agenda, she explained that her understanding of Jesus' teachings was that we were to love and accept everyone.

When I responded by challenging that those of us who oppose the dangerous lifestyle of homosexuality do so out of a sense of love, she reminded me that when confronted with the woman caught in adultery (another form of sexual indiscretion), Jesus warned only those who are without sin should cast the first stone. Tellingly, she decided to drop the period right in the middle of Jesus' sentence. Conveniently missing from Ms. Ritchie's defense was what Jesus went on to lovingly say to the prostitute: "Go and sin no more."[11]

And that was, after all, the heart of my question – is it possible for our society to satisfy the cries of "civil rights" for those practicing various forms of recreational sex while still providing for the rights of Christians to proclaim to those individuals, "go and sin no more?"

Though intentionally elusive and non-committal, her response contained enough substantive morsels to deduce the real answer: the two can coexist so long as Christians capitulate by neutering Scripture and accepting sin.

This is the painful reality that our society can continue to ignore, but that will continue pressing uncomfortably against us until we acknowledge its nagging presence. Our culture is being confronted with the choice of whether we will continue to protect the rights of conscience for Christians and other like-minded religious people, or if we will forsake those protections and instead create a right of sexual chaos where moral disapproval of any consensual sexual activity is forbidden. We simply can't have both.

As further evidence of this truth, consider a recent ruling from the United Kingdom's High Court. At issue was the foster care parenting rights not of practicing homosexuals, but of practicing Christians. Eunice and Owen Johns had applied to become foster parents, but were denied that right because of their religious conviction that homosexuality was deviant and immoral behavior.

The High Court saw this belief as discriminatory against homosexuals and thus deemed the Johns' home an improper environment for raising children. This is the danger in elevating behavior to the status of identity. By confusing homosexuality as who a person is rather than what a person does, moral disapproval of that behavior is removed from the concept of free opinion and placed in the category of condemnable hate.

The great irony, of course, is that by protecting practicing homosexuals from such discrimination, the High Court codified and condoned discrimination against practicing Christians. While they acknowledged the European Convention granted individuals a right to conscience and religion, the judges decided the degree to which Christianity is protected can be "qualified."

Got that? Religious rights now become "qualified" in order to allow for an unencumbered and unrestricted sexual license. Despite being built upon the framework of Western-Christian thought dating back to leading legal authorities, like the Scripturally devout Sir William Blackstone, the UK High Court exhibited no hesitation in choosing sides in this titanic struggle between the rights of conscience and the push for sexual anarchy.

They ruled, "While as between the protected rights concerning religion and sexual orientation there is no hierarchy of rights, there may, as this case shows, be a tension between equality provisions concerning religious discrimination and those concerning sexual orientation. Where this is so…the National Minimum Standards for Fostering and the Statutory Guidance indicate that it must be taken into account and in this limited sense the equality provisions concerning sexual orientation should take precedence."[12]

Though we've seen this imminent face-off between the demands of the aggressive sexual anarchists of the left and Christian rights of conscience brewing for some time – an Indianapolis cookie store threatened with eviction for declining to participate in a homosexual celebration,[13] a New Mexico photography business fined for declining to take pictures of a homosexual "ring ceremony,"[14] San Diego doctors taken to court for not providing a lesbian couple with in vitro fertilization,[15] evangelical dating site eHarmony.com bullied by the New Jersey Attorney General's Office into creating and operating a site for homosexuals[16] – this UK ruling is the most alarming development to date.

It indicates the uncompromisingly hostile position the left is taking towards traditional morality: one will win, the other will lose. To anyone paying attention, this antagonistic stance has been apparent from the infant days of the homosexual movement. In 1985, the homosexuality magazine *Advocate* editorialized: "The teaching that only male-female sexual activity within the bounds and constraints of marriage is the only acceptable form should be reason enough for any homosexual to denounce the Christian religion."[17]

And this creates one of the more peculiar ironies about the homosexual lobby that too many in our culture fail to notice. While shrewdly portraying Christians as intolerant bullies, even coining the label "homophobe" to shame them, these sexual anarchists actually commit the very offense they purport to be condemning.

For instance, as a public high school teacher, I have had a few encounters with the radical sexual group GLSEN (Gay, Lesbian, Straight Education Network). GLSEN touts itself as an organization designed to combat the bullying and mistreatment of students practicing homosexuality in public schools across America. Certainly, regardless of how you feel about the issue of homosexuality, school is a place where any student should feel safe, and be free of threats and intimidation.

This provides GLSEN a perfect façade to work its way into school systems across America, conducting their vaunted "Day of Silence" to raise awareness of the mistreatment of young people supposedly bullied into the shadows because of their sexual preferences.

But the reality of GLSEN is something quite different from its public image. My exposure in the classroom to GLSEN's materials has demonstrated that their interest is not in ending bullying, but rather redirecting the intimidation onto new targets - specifically, young children and teenagers who profess traditional moral values and who have been raised in Christian homes.

GLSEN's own curriculum guides for teachers advise them to - without parental knowledge or consent - question their students on the validity of their religious upbringing. Their tactics are to create an atmosphere where any objection to the practice of homosexuality (no matter how legitimate, loving, or reasoned that objection might be) is perceived as a threat of violence, and therefore must be dealt with by the school through disciplinary action. If that isn't bullying into silence, I don't know what is.

And age appropriateness is totally lost on GLSEN and its cronies. Besides handing out "ally cards" in kindergarten classrooms and providing recommended reading lists to schools that include some horrifically graphic sexual content, consider what occurred at GLSEN's annual student convention held at Tufts University in 2000. There, student attendees as young as 14 sat through sexually provocative sessions that involved discussion over homosexual oral sex and the depraved practice of "fisting." Does this not seem to fit perfectly with the depraved legacy of this movement's founder...Alfred Kinsey himself?

Though the conference was closed to media, undercover journalists managed to break the story by revealing a secretly recorded audio tape from one of these sex sessions. The resulting embarrassment was minimized because the national media is an ally of GLSEN and ignored the story entirely.

As a consequence, the 2001 conference was much of the same, with an estimated 400 student attendees being given a "fisting kit" of plastic gloves as well as "dental dams" for use during oral sex. In 2005, GLSEN was caught distributing gay "leather bar" guides to teens in attendance. Not only would it be illegal for many of these young people to even enter the bars, but with the indisputable prevalence of pedophilia in the male homosexual culture, these guides are nothing more than attempts to lure young people into extremely dangerous surroundings.

With as shocking as this may be, it shouldn't surprise us. This is the long-standing mantra of the sexual anarchists dating back to Kinsey: any kind of sex, any partner(s), anywhere, anytime. And anyone who has moral objections to such a philosophy is immediately portrayed as an oppressor, or hater of those who advocate it. This led to the following exchange I had with Barry, a self-described "homosexual" who called into my radio show:

> Barry: Live and let live, live and let live, Peter. I don't tell you your preferred sexual behavior is wrong, so why are you telling me mine is?

> Peter: Well, because it is.

> Barry: No, because you're a homophobe.

> Peter: And there it is.

> Barry: You are. You're a homophobe.

> Peter: Meaning I hate homosexuals?

Barry: Meaning, well yeah, you hate homosexuals. That's pretty apparent.

Peter: Okay, Barry, I want to address this. I want to address this. You are accusing me of something pretty outrageous here and I think this is important. My objections to homosexuality are born out of love, not hate.

Barry: Oh yeah. I'm sure that –

Peter: Just hold on, hold on, hold on. What is it to love someone?

Barry: You care about them. You want what's best for them.

Peter: Agreed. Now, Barry when I look at homosexuality from different angles, here's what I see. Physically the lifestyle is deadly. Some studies reveal a dramatically lowered life expectancy, and even if you reject those studies, you can't overcome the outrageously high preponderance of sexually transmitted diseases within the homosexual community. You're with me so far?

Barry: But it doesn't matter even if that's true-

Peter: Okay, but that's what I see from the physical side of homosexuality. From the psychological side, I see individuals who look for fulfillment and happiness in various depraved sexual activities, but never seem to find it. Depression is a hallmark of homosexuality. Promiscuity is the norm, not the exception. Even in states where homosexual "marriage" is legal, it doesn't seem to contribute to more stable relationships. That's psychological. Culturally, I see the frightening spread of disease, and increase in health care costs, and with as unsettling as this may be to you, the statistical significance between homosexuality and pedophilia is overwhelming.

Barry: Oh that's not true. Not all homosexuals are pedophiles. It's slander.

Peter: Never said they were. What I said was that the statistics show something beyond coincidence or even correlation. I've got a quote here in front of me from Dr. Brongersma writing in the Journal of Homosexuality and I'm just going to read it to you. He writes that parents shouldn't view a pedophile "as a rival or competitor, not as a thief of their property, but as a partner in the boy's upbringing, someone to be welcomed into their home." I've got all of the major homosexual publications – the Edge, Metroline, The Guide, Advocate, the San Francisco Sentinel – that have all editorialized in favor of pedophilia and sex with children. The North American Man-Boy Love Association was invited to participate in the 1993 Homosexual March on Washington. This isn't just coincidence. That is what the embrace of homosexuality is breeding culturally.

Barry: But you can't condemn all homosexuals for –

Peter: Hold on, please Barry, let me finish. We're not talking about condemning. We're talking about whether I'm a homophobe, whether I hate you and others who claim to be homosexual. Remember Barry, I'm a Christian. So on top of all of those realities – cultural and physical and emotional – I also look at the spiritual consequences of homosexuality.

Barry: Here we go.

Peter: Now wait. Whether you believe in it or not doesn't change the fact that I do. And I see that homosexuality is unquestionably condemned and that it isn't reconcilable with any understanding of Godly living. And I see in Scripture that those who engage in this lifestyle unrepentant will face the same dire consequences that any of us who don't repent of our sins will face. So add them up, Barry and answer me a question. Add them up, physically, emotionally, culturally, spiritually. When I see the tragic consequences of homosexuality, how would I show love to someone? Would I encourage someone to embrace those consequences or would I try to steer them clear of it? I'll tell you Barry, I think sadly you've got it backwards. The true homophobes are those who are telling you to embrace something as deadly as sexual depravity. The ones who love you are the ones who are willing to face the derision of fools and the criticism of our pop culture and try to knock that revolver out of your hand before you play this deadly game of Russian Roulette with your sexual behavior.

Barry: Well, sexual behavior isn't the same as playing a suicidal game. I mean-

Peter: The statistics seem to indicate otherwise, Barry.[18]

Barry was a nice guy who had been tragically misled by the deceptive voices of Kinsey's modern prophets. Voices like left-wing comedienne Joy Behar who leveled this tired accusation against mega-minister Joel Osteen who came onto the mind-numbing ABC program *The View* to promote a book: "When you say that the Bible is against gays, that makes people get bullied, and bad things happen to people because of what the people say about that."

Though not the most grammatically spectacular indictment, it is the same common refrain we hear from GLSEN and all the other sexual anarchists: if you don't agree with us, you're bullying us...particularly if you try to use the Bible as a defense of your position. What nonsense.

First, the Bible is not "against gays." The Bible condemns the activity of homosexuality, as well as many other sexually deviant behaviors. In fact, the Bible doesn't even recognize the existence of a group known as "gays." It acknowledges the existence of males and females, and the moral expectations for their sexual behavior (recognizing that behavior is always a choice).

Second, the Bible never commends or advocates bullying of any kind. Whether the Golden Rule, the fruit of the Spirit, or the parables of Christ himself, Christian principle teaches respect and dignity for all those made in the image of God.

Third, there is a profound difference between moral objection to the dangerous and deadly behavior of homosexuality and the physical intimidation or abuse of those tempted by same-sex attraction. Warning against and opposing the societal embrace of sexually deviant behavior is not bullying.

If it is, then our culture should express moral outrage at First Lady Michelle Obama and her Eat Right campaign to fight childhood obesity. Obviously her involvement with this crusade makes her complicit with the brutal bullying that takes place of obese children. After all, the most bullied group of young people in our country remains the overweight ones. Mrs. Obama's warning against the societal embrace of unhealthy eating habits is only ostracizing and stigmatizing the fat kids, thus inviting more bullying. And clearly her opposition to overeating couldn't be born out of love and concern for those kids' well being, could it?

I always thought that would be a great question to pose to her husband, President Barack Obama, given that he promoted GLSEN's founder, radical sexual anarchist Kevin Jennings to be the country's "Safe Schools Czar." And while he's answering, I could ask as a follow-up how leading kids towards deadly sexual behavior - something Mr. Jennings dedicated his life to - is promoting "safe schools?"

Sadly, those questions will never be asked because those in the media with the platform to ask them are Kinsey culture converts, dedicating themselves to promoting the normalization of each new rung in the sexual revolutionary ladder. From our movies to music, textbooks to television, we are bombarded with the imagery that tells us there is nothing better about "Mom and Dad," than "Mom and Mom," or "Dad and Dad." It's been the strategy from the beginning, as this November 1987 feature "Overhauling Straight America" in the homosexual Guide magazine proves:

> The first order of business is desensitization
> of the American public concerning gays and
> gay rights. To desensitize the public is to
> help it view homosexuality with indifference

instead of with keen emotion. Ideally, we would have straights register differences in sexual preferences the way they register different tastes for ice cream or sports games. At least in the beginning, we are seeking public desensitization and nothing more. We do not need and cannot expect a full 'appreciation' or 'understanding' of homosexuality from the average American. You can forget about trying to persuade the masses that homosexuality is a good thing. But if only you can get them to think that it is just another thing…then your battle for legal and social rights is virtually won.[19]

Think about that every time you allow your children to watch an episode of *Glee*, or a rerun of *Will and Grace*. And as odd or as difficult as it may be to grasp, the legacy of the sexual revolution teaches us that soon other sexual expressions will be following the same strategic path. Polygamy Day, Inc. already goes by the slogan, "Polygamy, the Next Civil Rights Battle." The trail has been forged and barring a cultural renewal, the same normalization campaign currently being applied to homosexuality will move on to other depraved acts like bestiality and incest. It's nothing more than the logical progression down the path towards sexual anarchy we have been following for decades.

When Kinsey started the fire, most resisted the idea that sex should be entertainment, until pop culture normalized it. Even then, most resisted the idea that divorce should be easily attainable, until pop culture normalized it. Even then, most resisted the idea that promiscuity should be celebrated, until pop culture normalized it. Even then, most resisted the idea that depraved activities like homosexuality and cross-dressing should be accepted, until pop culture normalized it. What comes next?

A paraphrase of Alexander Pope's haunting poem rings true:

> Evil is a monster of so frightful mien,
> As to be hated needs but to be seen.
> Yet seen too often, and familiar with her face,
> We first endure, then pity, then embrace.[20]

Could there be a more appropriate description of the silent encroachment sexual depravity has made into our culture and the destruction it is unleashing on the most important of our institutions, the family?

If nothing else, the mere fact that Satan would target the family unit with such a withering assault from both internal and external forces should reveal to us how vitally important it is to the preservation of any vibrant and prosperous society. History teaches us that healthy and happy families provide the surest supports to any people.

That is why any hope for cultural renewal demands that we, the 78, guard against the temptations that implode the family, resist the depravity that corrupts it, and defeat the humanist movement that seeks to transform it from its divinely given role in creation.

CHAPTER THIRTEEN

GETTING IT

Whenever I go to speak somewhere, I'm always leery about what kind of questions I will get afterwards. Because with as much as you know your topic, and as much as you've prepared, there will inevitably be someone who comes up with something that challenges you or that takes you off guard. That happened to me at a church in Muncie, Indiana after I concluded my four part series called *The Unmentionables*, which explains how Christians must respond to major cultural issues.

I was anticipating questions about the topics – abortion, capital punishment, homosexuality and pornography – but got something much different. As people filed past me following the final presentation, I noticed an older gentleman standing off to the side. It was quite apparent he had something weighing heavily on his mind. After the last person exited the auditorium, he came over, shook my hand and said, "I need to know something." When I asked him what, he said, "I need to know why you get it."

At first I wasn't really sure what he was asking, so I just stood there. Perhaps sensing my confusion he continued, "I had kids. They didn't end up like you. I have grandkids. They aren't going to end up like you. I need to know what it is that made you 'get it' when so many other young people your age are floating aimlessly or are actual enemies to the causes that we both know are right."

Nothing had prepared me for that question because I'd never been asked it before. It was in one way flattering, in another way intimidating. I appreciated that he evidently believed that I was passionately defending truth, but I certainly didn't feel qualified to expound upon the recipe for what caused that. And being acutely aware of your own failings and faults, it's an odd position to be put in when someone wants you to tell them how to make others end up like you. To be honest, I don't really remember my answer to him, but I doubt it was what he was looking for.

The truth is that I still don't know that there is a flawless formula to articulate because there are so many elements that contribute to "getting it." Certainly there is the Biblical admonition to "train up a child in the way he should go, and when he is old he will not depart from it."[1] But that verse entails a great deal. Training a child is obviously the primary responsibility of the parents, but we would be fools not to recognize that there are other entities that play a large part in either supplementing or contradicting the course those parents are attempting to chart.

Personally, I know that my parents helped immensely in setting my feet upon the straight and narrow path, and I will forever be grateful to them and to God for that. They took great pains to make sure I went to church, attended youth group and understood the need for Bible study. But while that went a long way in guiding the decisions I would later make, they couldn't make those decisions for me. I chose my friends, I chose my hobbies, and I chose what philosophies I would embrace and what ones I would reject.

And that's why any hope for cultural renewal depends upon us making some dramatic and landmark changes in our schools. Besides the home, there is no greater influence on the types of citizens our country produces than the classroom. In their most formative and impressionable years, many of our young people spend far more "quality" time (and by that I mean non-leisure) in school than they do at home. In other words, teachers and textbooks are going to have profound impacts on whether our kids grow up and "get it."

So how are we doing? Look around. Our society is an instructive reflection of what is happening in our school systems. With ten years' experience as a public high school teacher in what I regard as an excellent, exemplary district, I can testify to the fact that the deterioration of American society is directly related to some tragic flaws at the heart of our educational establishment. And – as I expressed from the opening chapters – we are completely misdiagnosing these flaws, pointing the finger at poor teachers, poor funding, poor facilities and poor management.

Unquestionably, specific districts would exhibit

one or a combination of all of those concerns. But the
problem is far more fundamental and far more
widespread than that. Therefore, any focus on those
issues alone will have at best a superficial impact on
correcting the underlying defect. That defect is a
warped starting point that attempts to separate Real
Morality and Christian ethics from education.

As I've explained previously, embracing and
advocating Christian ethics is something entirely
different than enforcing a strict religious code. Only an
addled mind could conclude that training children
from the earliest ages about the value of loving your
neighbor as yourself, doing unto others as you would
have them do unto you, being frugal, generous, self-
sacrificial and a good steward of creation somehow
amounts to inappropriate indoctrination of our youth.

Some will argue that those principles can be
taught, but it's the connection to Christianity that
makes them unsuitable for the classroom. Public
schools are funded by tax dollars, they argue, so
therefore it's unacceptable that there would be any
mention of a specific religion like Christianity as the
foundation point of those values. But by removing the
cornerstone of ethics, we destabilize and fatally wound
the entire structure. Those of my generation and
younger have first hand experience of this. We can
thank the warped leftist philosophy that demands
moral education be removed of any Christian
underpinnings for spawning the infamous self-esteem
movement we now firmly embrace in the American
school system.

Though it is woven into the curriculum
beginning in elementary school, my first real

experience with this "let's teach values but not mention any foundation for them" crusade came in a 7th grade class I had to take called, "Quest." It just sounds touchy-feely, doesn't it?

The class activities included getting in a circle, putting our names on a paper and then passing it around to every other student. Each person had to write something nice about everyone else on their respective paper. I think that was supposed to help us feel good about ourselves, but since every girl in the class wrote something like, "a good friend...I think of you as my little brother" on my paper, it was one whale of a disappointment.

We spent a majority of class time talking about our feelings, about trying to know the differences between right and wrong, and about self-esteem. In one disastrous exercise, we were each given a balloon and instructed to blow it up with air, but not to tie it off. We then went in front of the class with a partner and used scripts to simulate conversations that junior highers might have with one another in the hallways. If someone said something mean, we had to let a little bit of the air out of our balloons. By the end of the simulation, I'm guessing we were supposed to be moved by the sight of the fully inflated balloons of those who received compliments and the contrasting appearance of the droopy, deflated balloons of those who had been insulted. In actuality, what I remember is that we all got in trouble for trying to make human flatulence noises when we let air out of our balloons (what did they really expect from a bunch of junior high kids?).

In Quest (and all the other self-esteem

curriculum that is now out there), we can see the very dilemma of attempting to teach values without the fixed point-of-reference that Christianity offers. What, after all, is the basis of self-esteem? What is the basis of ethics? Think about the way those questions are answered in our schools today:

Teacher:	Kids, like we've told you, your life is nothing but a cosmic accident. You are nothing but a meaningless conglomeration of molecules that came together purely by chance billions of years ago. So ultimately, there is no meaning to your life. But that doesn't mean it's not valuable. Question, Jimmy?
Jimmy:	Yeah, if there's no meaning to life, then why is my life valuable?
Teacher:	Well look at everything you can do! You can contribute so much to our society. You can think and create and form things. You can run and jump and play. That's why you're valuable – take pride in those things! Yes, Jimmy?
Jimmy:	My brother was born with serious birth defects. He is in a wheelchair and can't do all those things you were talking

about. Does that mean his life isn't worth as much as mine? What gives his life meaning?

Teacher: Oh...yes...well, in that case your brother can feel good about himself because people appreciate him. Even if he can't do a bunch of things, there are still people that care about him, so that is what he can take pride in...that's what gives his life meaning. Yes Jimmy...another question?

Jimmy: Teacher, don't you know that my Dad left my family when he found out my brother was going to be such a challenge. We haven't heard from him in years. My Mom works three jobs just to try to make ends meet and she's never around. My brother and I have moved schools so many times and no one ever seems to notice that we're gone. I can guarantee he doesn't feel appreciated. I don't either. Does that mean he doesn't have meaning? Or at least it seems like his life isn't worth as much as others, right?

Teacher: Jimmy, seriously, sometimes you just can't look to others to give your life meaning…

Jimmy: I thought that's what you just told me to do?

Teacher: Don't interrupt. Sometimes when you can't find meaning from others, you have to look deep within yourself. As we've talked about, Maslow's "Hierarchy of Needs"[2] clearly shows that "self actualization" is the most important thing you can pursue. You want to find meaning, search within yourself Jimmy.

Jimmy: Uh…but I'm the one that's confused in the first place…how's that gonna help?

Teacher: Let's change the topic, shall we?

Jimmy: Okay. If, like you said, life has no meaning, then why is it bad to mistreat people?

Teacher: I don't understand what you're asking. Why would you want to mistreat people?

Jimmy: Maybe because they're annoying. Maybe because they pick on me. Maybe because I'm having a bad day and they cross me. Maybe because they're stupid. Maybe because they flaunt how privileged they are in front of me. I've got a lot of reasons why I'd like to mistreat people. What I'm wondering is if you have any reasons why I shouldn't?

Teacher: Jimmy, go to the office.

Do you see the problem we're facing? We tell kids to find the answers they need to define their existence within themselves but those answers aren't there. Why? Because we're not God. Kids should be told to find their sense of meaning outside their own obsessions, desires, feelings and wants. They should be told that self-esteem has nothing to do with self, but everything to do with an Authority that designed and created them each for a purpose, and despite their gifts or deficiencies, their talents or challenges, they have intrinsic worth that cannot be diminished or destroyed.

And besides being the foundation for self-esteem, they should be told that Authority provides a basis for ethics and values and is the ultimate standard by which our behavior can and will be judged. By not doing so, we cripple our children's character from the very beginning. And given that moral character is the linchpin of any meaningful "education," we totally undermine our school systems by depriving them of the ability to fuse concrete Real Morality with their teaching.

Think about it. We believe schools should focus

on scholarship. But making the most out of your academic opportunities, resources, and potential – which is scholarship – is a direct reflection of your character.

We believe schools should teach leadership skills. But grasping the difference between right and wrong, bringing others to a similar understanding, and guiding them in truth and honesty – which is leadership – is a direct reflection of your character.

We believe that schools should teach kids about service. But putting the interests, concerns, and needs of others ahead of your own prideful, selfish ambition – which is service – is a direct reflection of your character.

Everything we expect schools to do – from breeding academic excellence to fostering teamwork to developing sportsmanship – ultimately hinges on their ability to instill the critical and irreplaceable elements of moral character into young people. Founding Father Dr. Benjamin Rush understood why this had to be the supreme purpose of any meaningful teaching and learning:

> I beg leave to remark that the only foundation for a useful education in a republic is to be laid in religion. Without this, there can be no virtue, and without virtue there can be no liberty, and liberty is the object and life of all republican governments.[3]

In other words, our entire civilization is one built upon the premises of freedom, liberty and self-government. Since (as we have previously established) virtue is necessary for those things to endure, instilling morality should be the foremost objective of any national education system. And, as Rush observed, the best source from which we derive human morality is the religion of Christianity. He wrote:

> ...the religion I mean to recommend in this place is the religion of Jesus Christ.[4]

Any such recommendation today would be regarded as some diabolical scheme to indoctrinate young minds by turning the classroom into a sanctuary. Intentionally ignoring and publicly disregarding the self-evident distinction between compelling students into the Christian faith (evangelizing, baptizing, offering communion) and instilling Christian principle into their hearts and minds (things like patience, love, kindness, gentleness, self control), the modern humanist left has spent decades chasing Christianity from the government school system.

There's no question what their purpose is in doing so. Rather than attempt to fight a futile battle to "de-Christianize" the country by arguing with 78% of the population, these humanists have sought to use the schools to proselytize their own beliefs and make converts out of each new generation. The founder of the first Humanist Society of New York, Charles F. Potter, explained the strategy:

> Education is thus a most powerful ally of Humanism, and every American public school is a school of Humanism. What can the theistic Sunday-schools, meeting for an hour once a week, and teaching only a

fraction of the children, do to stem the tide of
a five-day program of humanistic teaching?[5]

It is apparent that humanists like Potter
understand that, "The philosophy of the schoolroom in
one generation will be the philosophy of government in
the next." Though the authorship of that quote is a
matter of some debate, its source is ultimately
immaterial given that the principle it espouses is
largely true. What we teach our kids to value today
will be what our government and culture value
tomorrow – a reality that perfectly explains what is
occurring in our schools at the behest of modern
atheist/humanist academics.

By taking over the curriculum of our school
system and eliminating through court order any
reference to the Judeo-Christian ethic in educational
materials, the humanist left wars against Christian
principle in our schools with a ruthless efficiency. They
create false dichotomies and then embed them into the
minds of impressionable children.

For instance, they intentionally obliterate any
rational basis for a belief in a Creator by perpetuating
the myth that on the question of origin, we can choose
faith or science. This intellectually dishonest assertion
indoctrinates young people that, "you can believe fairy
tales if you want to, but the science unquestionably
proves the humanist explanation for the existence of
the universe." Hardly.

Leaving aside the insurmountable scientific
hurdles facing any molecules-to-man evolutionary
miracle, leaving aside the falsified research and
disproven hoaxes that Darwinists still perpetuate in

textbooks, leaving aside the embarrassing defense of such unscientific fantasies like spontaneous generation and the Big Bang (aka "First there was nothing, then it exploded"), leaving aside the unmistakable fingerprint of design that exists on everything from massive galaxies to the smallest protozoa, this amounts to an inexcusable betrayal of the very definition of science.

Science proves what we see and observe. But what is going on behind that which we see and observe is far more about philosophy than it is science. It's far more about our presuppositions and yes, faith…than it is fact. Given that no one observed the beginning of all things, we ultimately have no scientific way to prove what occurred. That means, in the final analysis, what we are left with is not a battle of faith vs. science, but faith vs. faith. Even Nobel winning evolutionist Harold Urey acknowledged as much when he wrote,

> All of us who study the origin of life find that the more we look into it, the more we feel that it is too complex to have evolved anywhere. We all believe as an article of faith that life evolved from dead matter on this planet.[6]

Now, we can certainly follow the evidence, but even that is subject to interpretations that are governed by our biases and presuppositions. This was perfectly illustrated a couple years ago after two seemingly mutually exclusive scientific finds were reported.

In late April of 2010, news reports surfaced from Turkey that a team of evangelical researchers had claimed to find the remains of Noah's Ark on Mount Ararat.[7] The team confirmed that they were "99.9 percent" sure that the wooden structure they found was part of the Biblical vessel that preserved life during the cataclysmic flood approximately 5,000 years ago.

Within moments of their announcement, evolutionary scientists began to cast doubt on the find. The headline at MSNBC read, "Noah's Ark Found? Not so Fast."[8] Stories appeared, quoting archaeologists like Peter Kuniholm from Cornell who called the reported find a "crock."[9] Paul Zimansky, an archaeologist and historian at Stony Brook University who specializes in that region of the world, dismissed the reports as well, stating, "Press releases are not the way archaeology advances."[10]

Though I certainly agree with that sentiment, I have to wonder where Zimansky and these other critics were less than a year earlier when another earth-shattering discovery was touted by media reports. Then, rather than being a potential find that would go a long way to validate the Biblical record of history (and by extension the creationist model), it was the reported discovery of the so-called Darwinian missing link.

Nicknamed "Ida," this perfectly preserved lemur-like fossil was said to provide the, "final piece of Darwin's jigsaw." But unlike the supposed Ark discovery, the frenzy that ensued from this press release was far from skeptical.

Sky News called it, "the eighth wonder of the world."[11] National Geographic trumpeted that Ida was a "branching point on the evolutionary tree."[12] British naturalist David Attenborough proclaimed, "The link, they would have said until now, is missing. Well, it is no longer missing."[13] ABC's Good Morning America showcased the fossil. Both the History Channel and BBC One aired documentaries on Ida called, "The

Link." A book by the same title was published almost instantaneously. Even the online search engine Google fell prey to the trap and modified its search page banner to depict Ida. Within a week, over 630 online news sites had covered the groundbreaking story.

A year on, the scientific community was recognizing that there was nothing very special about Ida after all. Well, perhaps that's not fair. The remarkable preservation of the lemur-like creature was stunning (something best explained by a rapid burial in sediment...sort of like what would happen in a catastrophic worldwide flood). But all those references to Ida as a "missing link" were summarily removed from the final scientific paper by the conscientious peer-review process.

So why the two different standards? Why does the potential find of Noah's Ark generate scorn and immediate skepticism if the potential find of the "missing link" does not? By the way, though I certainly believe in Noah's flood, I should acknowledge that I think the skepticism over the Ark find is completely appropriate. Every couple years it seems, a new group claims to have found it - and usually the evidence is less than compelling, as was the case with this particular "discovery" in question. But what we should be asking is how that is any different from the missing link - something that Darwin's modern prophets angrily say has already been found until a news story like Ida reveals the truth that they are desperately still searching for it?

The truth is that science is supposed to be skeptical of everything. And yet so often we see the reality that Darwinists hijack the name of science in an effort to proselytize their own faith, and thereby commit the same offense they condemn creationists for perpetrating. Think about it:

Kuniholm mocked the Ark hunters by saying, "These guys have already gotten the answer worked out ahead of time, and then they go out to prove it."[14] In other words, if there does end up being a large wooden structure on the mountain, that doesn't necessarily prove Noah's story. It only proves there is something wooden on the mountain. Creationists then work that structure into a narrative they've already accepted of a worldwide flood.

Fair enough. But what was Ida? Nothing about her suggested anything other than an extinct, lemur-like creature. Yet, Darwinists took a dead organism and worked it into a narrative they've already accepted of macro-evolution. They presuppose Darwin's model is correct and then interpret the fossil in a way that helps tell the story.

So how about some intellectual honesty? Science can prove there's a wooden structure on a mountain and a dead lemur in the rocks. But how we choose to interpret those scientific facts is much more about our presuppositions and faith than it is science. And that's true on both sides.

But thanks to Supreme Court rulings like *Edwards v. Aguillard*[15] in 1987, only one side can be legally presented to students. However, if there are only two theories on origin, both of which are ultimately rooted in faith, and the state forbids one from being discussed while demanding the other be taught exclusively, do we not have the official state establishment of one religious view? Is this not a violation of the precious "separation of church and state" doctrine?

It would be if the doctrine was a serious attempt to bring fairness and equity to the classroom. But of course it's not. The left does not bristle when students are required to read Homer's *Iliad* and *Odyssey* which sing the praises of the gods of Greek mythology. They don't recoil when students are exposed to Emerson and Thoreau's religions of romanticism and transcendentalism. They don't bat an eye when students encounter the atheist proclivities of Karl Marx in sociology class. In fact in some cases, the same leftist intellectuals who vehemently demand separation of anything remotely Christian from schools actually condone and approve the fusing of other religions with classroom activity. Consider what happened in California in 2006:

> In a recent federal decision that got surprisingly little press, even from conservative talk radio, California's 9th U.S. Circuit Court of Appeals ruled it's OK to put public-school kids through Muslim role-playing exercises, including:
>
> - Reciting aloud Muslim prayers that begin with "In the name of Allah, Most Gracious, Most Merciful . . . ."
>
> - Memorizing the Muslim profession of faith: "Allah is the only true God and Muhammad is his messenger."
>
> - Chanting "Praise be to Allah" in response to teacher prompts.

- Professing as "true" the Muslim belief that "The Holy Quran is God's word."

- Giving up candy and TV to demonstrate Ramadan, the Muslim holy month of fasting.

- Designing prayer rugs, taking an Arabic name and essentially "becoming a Muslim" for two full weeks.

Parents of seventh-graders, who after 9-11 were taught the pro-Islamic lessons as part of California's world history curriculum, sued under the First Amendment ban on religious establishment. They argued, reasonably, that the government was promoting Islam.

But a federal judge appointed by President Clinton told them in so many words to get over it, that the state was merely teaching kids about another "culture."

So the parents appealed. Unfortunately, the most left-wing court in the land got their case. The 9th Circuit, which previously ruled in favor of an atheist who filed suit against the words "under God" in the Pledge of Allegiance, upheld the lower court ruling.[16]

Do you suppose if I began teaching a curriculum unit in my classes that required students to take on a Christian name, pray through Christ, take communion and be baptized in the high school pool that the ACLU and our federal courts would give me a pass? Obviously not. So why the different standard?

In my experiences in the classroom, no one has ever questioned why I have Marx's *Communist Manifesto*, Hitler's *Mein Kampf,* or Darwin's *Origin of Species* on my bookshelves. But the moment they see the Bible on my desk, the first question they ask: "Is that legal?" How sad.

And yet also how revealing about what we are witnessing. The separation doctrine, much like the false dichotomy of faith vs. science, is utilized by the humanist left solely as a battering ram to obliterate Christianity from the school system. Darwinist G. Richard Bozarth explained the objective this way:

> And how does a god die? Quite simply because all his religionists have been converted to another religion, and there is no one left to make children believe they need him. Finally, it is irresistible – we must ask how we can kill the god of Christianity. We need only insure that our schools teach only secular knowledge…If we could achieve this, God would indeed be shortly due for a funeral service.[17]

The problem with our schools sending God to the morgue, however, should at this point be fairly obvious to all of us. Without a proper recognition of the foundation point for the values our culture depends upon for its survival, those preparing to take the reins of our society will be unable to articulate, or even appreciate, what sets Western civilization apart from all of the others.

That, of course, is the left's ultimate goal. Once the foundations have been destroyed, and once the mystique of our Western traditions has worn thin, the ground is fertile for the cultural transformation they have been so long pursuing. If we are to resist it, we had best become wise to their strategy – one that focuses less on arguing with us, while concentrating more on training our children in the way they want them to go.

CHAPTER FOURTEEN

TAKING BACK THE CLASSROOM

Every year on the first day of my American history and American government classes, I give my high school students a test. They love tests...especially the first day of school. The questions are meant to gauge their knowledge of the subject matter so I have a decent idea of what I'm working with that semester. After ten years, I am considering suspending this practice, not because I don't find it a helpful or useful exercise, but because it's becoming too depressing.

It is not uncommon for foreign exchange students to score higher on the test than the rest of the class. This typically elicits embarrassed laughs, but never the dramatic soul-searching it would seem to provoke. Most high school students I have encountered are good kids with good hearts, good attitudes and good intentions. Their casual and complacent mindset is more than anything a product of our nation's prosperity.

They simply can't imagine a world without cell phones, fast food, and three family vehicles. To them those things aren't blessings, bur rather essentials. They seemingly didn't require any real sacrifice to obtain, but simply came as a birthright and entitlement. Most of our young people think poverty is defined by food stamps and public housing with nothing beyond basic cable. Call them spoiled if you want, but they don't mean to take our unimaginable wealth and privilege for granted; they just don't know any better.

That our schools are not doing a more conscientious job teaching the next generation the unique heritage and traditions that have led to American greatness is not only a travesty, it is a grave mistake. Author John Steinbeck explained why:

> Now we face the danger which in the past has been the most destructive to the human: success–plenty, comfort, and ever-increasing leisure. No dynamic people has ever survived these dangers. If the anesthetic of satisfaction were added to our hazards, we would not have a chance of survival–as Americans.[1]

America is distinct and exceptional. Our success is unmatched and our prosperity is unrivaled. This isn't due to some unnatural stroke of good luck or an advantageous roll of the dice. It's the direct result of our foundations; which is precisely why one of the primary objectives of the American school system should be to perpetuate those foundations and the values that provide the soil in which they are anchored.

Instead, thanks to an overriding anti-American

bias dominating the ivory towers of academia, a new generation of Americans is learning a retouched, refigured, and at times completely fabricated history of their country. History has become more about advancing ideology than an accurate recounting of past events.

The late Marxist storyteller Howard Zinn (dubbing Zinn an historian is an affront to those who take the profession seriously) epitomized this type of historical malpractice in his thoroughly discredited magnum opus, *A People's History of the United States*. Zinn himself admitted, "I wanted my writing of history and my teaching of history to be a part of social struggle…so that kind of attitude towards history, history itself as a political act, has always informed my writing and my teaching." Yet despite this admission of flagrant bias, many colleges and universities – as well as high schools – across America require Zinn's pseudo-history for the completion of some academic courses.

I initially encountered *A People's History* when I was a first year teacher. A friend had recommended that I read the book, "for a different perspective." Admittedly, I initially struggled to even take it seriously. As Dan Flynn questions in his scathing review of Zinn's work, what kind of a history text has no documentation and footnotes? What kind of American history text leaves out Washington's Farewell Address and Lincoln's Gettysburg Address, leaves out the moon landing and D-Day, leaves out Alexander Graham Bell and the Wright brothers…but makes plenty of room for Joan Baez and the Berrigan brothers?[2]

Zinn saw both the writing and teaching of history not as what it is: a noble profession bearing responsibility to transmit an accurate retelling of past events to new generations, but rather as a weapon to use in advancing a social and political agenda. Announcing that "objectivity is impossible…and it is also undesirable," Zinn attempted to absolve himself of any duty to honestly portray the events of the past. What resulted was the worst kind of revisionism that only the ignorant or indoctrinated could embrace:

Maoist China – the most murderous state in human history – is praised as the closest thing to a "people's government" China has known; the oppressive Sandinistas in Nicaragua were "welcomed"; Castro's Cuba "had no bloody record of suppression"; the American revolution was a clever trick by the Founders to ensure oppression of Americans; emancipation of the slaves was motivated only by greed; America, not Japan, was responsible for the attack on Pearl Harbor.[3]

Following its initial printing, respected historian Oscar Handlin dismantled Zinn's book in a review as being "deranged…fairy tales."[4] Yet, regardless of his shoddy methodology, apparently non-existent research, and glaring bias, Zinn has become a cultural hero for the American left. They see his as the voice that gives historical justification to what they have always believed about America: that she is a force of oppression and subjugation, a country whose success is the product not of divine principles, but of coercion and domination.

How successful have they been in transmitting this view to our children? With the support of a sympathetic media and an entertainment community in Hollywood determined to reinforce and amplify their message, more successful than you might believe. The last question I ask my students on their pre-course test is for them to give their general opinion of the United States of America. Few classes see anything better than 50% responding favorably about their country.

America's unique place in the world is being threatened from within. While we complacently enjoy the blessings of liberty passed down to us, we have welcomed into our schools a Trojan Horse full of leftist multiculturalists who are systematically undermining our Judeo-Christian heritage and thus destroying the foundation of our great success.

American exceptionalism has been replaced by their dangerously flawed premise that all ideas and beliefs are equally valid and good. This is the heart of the humanist left's message and why they feel it incumbent upon them to persistently diminish the greatness and goodness of America and its Christian underpinnings.

By obsessing over the inevitable flaws and failures of fallen men, the left hopes to convince impressionable minds that Christian thought produces no more productive or honorable consequences than other belief systems. Given the boatloads of historical evidence that contradicts that hypothesis, however, the left many times must overcompensate by exaggerating the supposed evils of Christianity and ignoring the full context of the sins they condemn.

For instance, while humanist scholars point to the devastating reality of slavery in America as evidence of the failure of Christian principle, they ignore that slavery still persists in non-Christian cultures. They disregard the significant reality that whether it was William Wilberforce in England, or Abraham Lincoln in the United States, the justification for ending the barbaric practice was based ultimately in Christian truth. They may be right that the men who authored the Declaration of Independence did not live up to the eternal truths therein. But intellectual honesty demands an acknowledgement that when Lincoln stated his case for ending the practice, he referenced "the proposition that 'all men are created equal'"[5] – one unquestionably rooted in Christian principle.

Consider also the treatment Spanish Christian conqueror Christopher Columbus receives from the modern left. While historians like Glenn Morris tag Columbus, "a murderer, a rapist, [and] architect of a policy of genocide that continues today," American Indian activist Russell Means puts it more succinctly: "Columbus makes Hitler look like a juvenile delinquent."[6] But beyond just Columbus, this is again meant to be a condemnation of the "brutality" of colonialism that emerged from Christian thought. In an insightful analysis that lays waste to such accusations, author and scholar Dinesh D'Souza exposes the underlying irony in the left's position:

> The West even supplied the Americas with a doctrine of human rights that would provide the basis for a sustained critique of Western colonialism. We may join [these critics]…in expressing outrage at the wanton Western seizure of Indian lands and abuses of basic rights. But upon reflection we would have to

admit that these criticisms depend upon concepts of property rights and human rights that are entirely Western. Long before Columbus, Indian tribes raided each other's land and preyed on the possessions and persons of more vulnerable groups. What distinguished Western colonialism was neither occupation nor brutality but a countervailing philosophy of rights that is unique in human history.[7]

This is profound. What this essentially means is that the left would be unable to criticize the behavior of these Christians if it were not for the Christian ethic of rights and fairness those same men brought to the continent.

Later, in his book *What's So Great About America*, D'Souza identifies the same phenomenon regarding the anti-colonialist movements in places like his home country of India, who sought independence from Western rule. While leftists point to the discriminatory colonial conquests as an indictment of the European Christians who perpetrated them, D'Souza tells the rest of the story:

> One of my high-school teachers in India liked to say, "If Hitler had been ruling India, Gandhi would be a lamp shade." This man was not known for his sensitivity, but he had a habit of speaking the truth. His point was that the success of Gandhi and of the Indian protestors, who prostrated themselves on the train tracks, depended on the certain knowledge that the trains would stop rather than run over them. With tactics such as

these, Gandhi and his followers hoped to
paralyze British rule in India, and they
succeeded. But what if the British had
ordered the trains to keep going? This is
certainly what Hitler would have done. I
don't see Genghis Khan or Attila the Hun
being deterred by Gandhi's strategy. Even as
the Indians denounced the West as wholly
unprincipled and immoral, they relied on
Western principles and Western morality to
secure their independence.[8]

Think of it this way: without the Christian
principle brought by the European colonialists which
introduced and infused the concept that man is
designed by his Creator for a specific purpose, freedom
and liberty would most likely have never come to those
parts of the world.

The principles, the ethics and values coming
from Judeo-Christian thought are superior. They are
better. History teaches repeatedly and without
contradiction that they are more beneficial and
conducive to producing a happy and prosperous
society. D'Souza knows it. Our Founders knew it.
And our children should be taught it in our schools.

We need not transform our public education
system into Bible schools that teach nothing but Biblical
precept in order to accomplish it. Nor need we violate
any Constitutional principle or infringe upon the rights
of every individual to worship freely and by the
dictates of their own conscience to accomplish it. We
need only to begin infusing the recognition of Moral
Authority with our public school curriculum.

Students should know that there is a transcendent moral authority that presides over the destinies of men and of nations. They should know that they are accountable in this life and the next for their actions. They should know that character matters above all else – that it defines them. And they should know that character is reflected not in how athletic or talented they are, but in how they use their God-given life to study, serve and sacrifice for others.

They should know that they are responsible for themselves, and that they have been given great freedom to make the most of their opportunities. They should know that their bodies are temples to be treated with the utmost respect and dignity as they bear the likeness of their Creator. They should know that justice is an eternal imperative that they cannot escape or ignore. They should know that while perfection can never be reached in a fallen world, we hold the privilege of committing ourselves to a relentless pursuit of imitating One who was.

They should know that some ideas are better than others, and that pretending otherwise is to invite calamity. They should know the reason why after studying all belief systems from ancient to modern times, and given the opportunity to implement any of them as the basis of our civilization, our Founders chose the Judeo-Christian model. They should know why Muslims find it safer to live in a country founded upon Christian principle than one rooted in the tenets of Islam. They should know why atheists find it safer to live in a country founded upon a belief in a Moral Authority than in one established on the idea that man is his own god.

These principles are already being taught in private schools, academies, and home school networks across America. It's why as a public school teacher I am such a vocal proponent of each of those, despite the objections of the heavy-handed teachers' unions who see these entities as their "competitors." That perception sadly reveals the reality of what these unions seem to value most: money. Their primary purpose has become securing as much money and benefits as possible for their members, regardless of any negative impact that may have on students. Since private schools and home schools threaten to diminish that money by enticing students away from the public system, they become the enemy.

But beyond just money issues, the commitment national teachers' unions like the National Education Association have made to promoting left-wing, anti-Christian causes represents another reason why they treat alternatives to public schools in an increasingly hostile fashion. Take, for example, the heartwarming moment elicited a few years ago when the NEA's retiring General Counsel Bob Chanin took to the stage at the group's annual convention to deliver his outgoing remarks.

There, with teachers, representatives, and affiliates all looking on, Chanin offered his inspiring and uplifting message that asserted the profound commitment held by the NEA to the betterment of American society: "We are not paranoid, someone really is after us. Why are these conservative and right-wing bas**rds picking on NEA and its affiliates? I will tell you why: it is the price we pay for success."[9]

As one of those right-wing "fatherless lads" Mr. Chanin was referring to, I found myself moved at how open-minded and inclusive his speech sounded. But more than that, Chanin did a masterful job of demonstrating what the true priorities of the NEA are when he stated that what makes the group effective is, "not because of our creative ideas, it is not because of the merit of our positions, it is not because we care about children, and it is not because we have a vision of a great public school for every child. NEA and its affiliates are effective advocates because we have power."[10]

Now there's a relief. Perhaps the NEA should put that quote on its promotional fliers? After all, who would want the largest association representing teachers in the country to be basing its effectiveness on its ability to improve the lives of children?! Thankfully, the leadership of the NEA has sought a pursuit of raw political power instead. And why are they so successful in this pursuit? Mr. Chanin explained, "And we have power because there are more than 3.2 million people who are willing to pay us hundreds of millions of dollars in dues each year."[11] Keep in mind that many of those 3.2 million are faithful Christian teachers who, though they seem to turn Mr. Chanin's stomach, are to just look the other way and continue sending in their money.

Sadly, the pathetic reality of the current state of affairs in the National Education Association gets worse. Besides throwing their full support behind homosexual "marriage" initiatives and using their resources and political muscle to advance the "right to choose abortion," the NEA actively champions anti

American causes.

How else can you explain the plan that appeared on the NEA's "Diversity Calendar" instructing teachers to make October 1st a special recognition of the Communist revolution in China?[12]   The NEA recommended teachers celebrate how the world's most notorious butcher, Chairman Mao Zedong, proclaimed the "Chinese people have stood up," as he established the regime that would slaughter more innocent human beings than any other in world history. After a public outcry, the NEA removed this item from their site.

But they left their recommended reading page for teachers, where they tout the work of self-proclaimed Satanist Saul Alinsky. In calling Alinsky, "an inspiration to anyone contemplating action in their community,"[13] the NEA encourages those charged with educating our children to immerse themselves in the tactics of progressive community organizing. They heartily endorse Alinsky's 1971 book, "Rules for Radicals" – a socialist how-to guide for gaining power and redistributing wealth.

As commentator Brannon Howse accurately observed, "The NEA is a group of radicals who are opposed to parental authority, opposed to accountability, and they're not for traditional education…They are for a progressive, liberal, anti-American worldview."[14] It's why the NEA applauds the work of communists like John Dewey and domestic terrorists like Bill Ayers, all the while publishing guides on how to defeat the "religious right."

With this group being the largest, most active, most influential organization affecting the direction of our public schools today, our responsibility becomes clear. Christians must flood and overrun the public school system.

Christians must run for school board offices and seek administrative posts, putting ourselves in the most advantageous position for influencing the direction of our schools. We must volunteer to serve on textbook adoption committees and fundamentally reject any book with the abusive strain of humanist propaganda woven throughout its pages. We must fill paraprofessional roles, teacher assistant jobs, library staffs, cafeteria positions and hall monitor openings, shining the light of Christian truth in every corner of the complex. We should be leading PTAs and extra-curricular clubs, directly influencing the content of what our schools promote. We should be applying for coaching positions and music program volunteer opportunities to make lasting impacts on the young people in whom we trust our future.

And most of all, we should be snatching up every teaching job available, prying loose the death grip of the NEA and its affiliates by systematically bleeding them of the dues money that brings them life. Simply put, there is no excuse for any American teacher (Christian or not) who believes in the values and principles of Western civilization to remain associated with the NEA. They are a culturally Marxist organization that holds a flagrant antipathy towards this country and its traditions. Any hope for cultural renewal demands that we neutralize their power, as well as that of their slightly less numerous counterparts at the American Federation of Teachers.

Some suggest that should be done by taking our Christian kids and evacuating the public schools. And while as a Dad I certainly understand the prerogative and authority of every concerned parent to do so (and would never criticize one who did), we adult Christians cannot take the same path. Even if we choose to home school or send our child to a private academy, we ourselves must not abandon the public system. Because the reality is that whether we like it or not, the public schools will continue to educate the vast majority of our youth for an indefinite amount of time. By removing our influence then, we hand the keys of our culture's future over to those who eagerly seek to take them and drive us off a cliff.

Rather than retreating from the schools, what the 78 need to employ is a surge strategy. Overrun the system and fill it. Once there, embedded behind the walls of our schools, we become (once again) the voice of the American classroom.

And if this seems too implausible a plan, consider that it is the very strategy the NEA and its fellow left-wing humanist allies fear most, as evidenced by their own words. Back in 1996, the NEA issued a handbook on dealing with the "radical right's crusade against public schools." The handbook states, "They won't go away. No matter how bizarre we believe their beliefs to be, no matter how illogical and inconsistent their goals appear, and no matter how often we reassure ourselves that 'this too, shall pass,' the political, social, and religious forces that make up the radical right in contemporary American society will not go away."[15]

When people ask me why as a Christian I continue laboring in a public school environment that is increasingly hostile to Christianity, I show them that

quote. I tell them that it is too important a task, and
this is too critical a moment for us to shrink back. Not
everyone is meant to be a teacher, and there may come
a day when God calls me to a different profession. But
we ignore at our own peril the momentous battle
raging in our public schools for the hearts and minds of
the next generation.

Our adversaries acknowledge it. Humanist John
Dunphy's now infamous quotation proves that:

> I am convinced that the battle for
> humankind's future must be waged and won
> in the public school classroom by teachers
> who correctly perceive their role as the
> proselytizers of a new faith: a religion of
> humanity…These teachers must embody the
> same selfless dedication as the most rabid
> fundamentalist preachers. For they will be
> ministers of another sort, utilizing a
> classroom instead of a pulpit to convey
> humanist values in whatever subject they
> teach, regardless of the educational level –
> preschool day care or large state university.[16]

The humanists' strategy is unambiguous and
aggressive. Ours must be no different.

They seek to turn the public school classroom
into the Garden of Eden, and hand the lectern over to
the ancient serpent to whimper out the eternal deceit
that ruins lives and ensures cultural misery: "ye shall
be as gods."[17]

We must seek to preserve the classroom as an
instrument that either supplements the eternal truth
spoken by righteous parents, or that supplies this truth

to those who tragically haven't heard it at home: "there is a God, and you aren't Him."

PART FIVE
THE REBIRTH

I am only one, but I am one. I cannot do everything, but I can do something. What I can do I should do, and with the help of God, I will do.

— *Everett Hale*

CHAPTER FIFTEEN

SONS OF ISSACHAR

Far too few Christians are familiar with the inspiring story of William Wilberforce. Despite the fame of the movie *Amazing Grace* that chronicled his tireless efforts in overcoming seemingly insurmountable odds to single handedly bring an end to the brutal slave trade in Britain, his name is largely unknown in the modern Christian lexicon.

Even those who know his story often fail to grasp how close it came to never happening. Upon his conversion to Christ, the talented orator and statesman Wilberforce wrestled in serious contemplation whether he should leave the worldly profession of politics to enter the full time ministry. Painfully agonizing over the path that God was calling him to, *Amazing Grace* depicts the fateful scene that sends chills down my spine every time I watch it. During a tense and anxious meeting with a handful of colleagues, a woman leans forward and, looking straight at Wilberforce, breaks the uncomfortable silence by persuading, "We understand you're having some trouble deciding whether to do the work of God or the work of a political activist. We humbly suggest, you can do both."

Who knows how many hundreds of thousands of slaves were spared the inhuman whip because of that powerful truth? Similarly, who knows the darkness that could be driven from our culture if we found the moral courage to embrace it today?

I'm always intrigued when I visit a church and hear the congregation sing the old hymn, "I Surrender All." Its refrain is so simple and yet so profound:

> I surrender all.
> I surrender all.
> All to Jesus, I surrender;
> I surrender all.

Often times I stand there listening to the voices echoing off the walls and wonder how many of us truly mean those words, or if to be more honest we should alter them ever so slightly, and sing:

> I surrender all...but my politics.
> I surrender all...but my music and television.
> All but my finances, I surrender;
> I surrender...my Sunday mornings.

God encompasses the totality of what is. There is no issue, no circumstance, no topic or situation where His truth is not applicable or important. And therefore, there must be no issue, circumstance, topic or situation where Christians are silent. But for whatever the reason – fear, intimidation, passivity, complacency, apathy or ignorance – silence is quickly becoming the defining quality of Christianity in America. Given a spirit of power and strength, we have exchanged it for one of timidity and have withdrawn from the front lines, ceding far too much ground in our culture.

So what must we do?

During my senior year of high school, I thought I had limited my choices of colleges down to either Northwestern University or Taylor University. That was before I agreed to go with my best friend to Indiana Wesleyan University on a visitation day. I immediately fell in love with that small, liberal arts campus. Of course, the fact that the institution was only a half hour away from my house didn't hurt either – I could live on campus but still bring my laundry home on weekends...jackpot.

But what truly convinced me to attend IWU was sitting in on one of Dr. Glenn Martin's classes while I was there visiting. His passion for understanding and illuminating the Biblical expectation for Christians to be the salt of the earth and light of the world was intoxicating.

For four years, I took every course the man offered. And in every one, he ended class by encouraging us to be "sons of Issachar." I'll admit that while I was impressed by his profound thinking and teaching, I never cared much about this monotonous and seemingly daily admonition. I knew Issachar was an Old Testament figure, and so I assumed he was telling us to be wise or strong in our faith. I was more concerned with getting out the door and on to lunch than actually taking the time to figure it out.

My second year out of college, I received word

via email that Dr. Martin had been diagnosed with a brain tumor and was not in good shape. By the time I got over to visit him in the hospital, he was in a coma and therefore I was never able to ask him what he meant by that phrase. I imagine that if I had, he would have told me to look it up for myself anyway. And so I did.

There is but one small, seemingly insignificant Scripture reference to the "sons of Issachar" that comes in the book of 1 Chronicles, chapter 12, verse 32: "And of the children of Issachar, which were men that had understanding of the times, to know what Israel ought to do…"[1]

As I look around American culture today, I realize why Dr. Martin so adamantly pressed this point. What I see is a society that is embracing evil and calling it good. I see a culture that kills its children and calls it choice. I see a culture that embraces depravity and calls it expression. I see a culture that celebrates perversion and calls it tolerance. I see a culture that excuses violence and calls it compassion. I see a culture that misleads and confuses its children and calls it education. I see a culture that destroys its own foundations and calls it multiculturalism. I see a culture that honors greed and calls it ambition.[2]

And rather than taking appropriate measures to counter this march into moral oblivion, our government has been overrun by those who lack either the will or the understanding of how to stop it. Cowardly, they hide behind a warped and perverted reading of the separation of church and state doctrine to excuse either their allegiance to immorality or their spineless neglect in confronting it.

And most catastrophic of all, as our culture inches perilously close to the knife-edge of calamity, our churches appear impotently disinterested in awakening the confused and corrupt to the impending disaster. Or worse, seeking the applause of men rather than the applause of heaven, they have themselves exchanged the truth of God for a lie.

I sat in astonishment watching a YouTube clip of Reverend Ed Bacon appearing on Oprah Winfrey's syndicated television show. Though aware of the fact that Oprah had long since dedicated her efforts to promulgating a do-it-yourself blend of new age, humanistic spiritualism, I was shocked to hear a supposed minister of the Gospel convey a message to millions of viewers that called for the acceptance of sin.

After having created a firestorm by stating on a prior show that, "being 'gay' is a gift from God,"[3] Reverend Bacon had returned to Oprah's program to clarify his remarks. He reasserted his outlandish claim by arguing, "God sent Jesus into the world not to condemn the world, but through Him all the world might be saved. You have to take that orientation, the orientation of compassion and inclusion to the Bible, or you're going to have to use it as a way to beat people up and condemn them and judge them."

Had Oprah honestly been interested in pursuing truth, she would have asked Reverend Bacon this simple question: "If Jesus came into the world to save the world, as you say, might I ask...save it from what?" For it is at that point that Reverend Bacon's position literally implodes. Jesus came into the world to save people from sins. He did it by offering them redemption for those sins, provided that they would repent of their wrongdoing. That is why Jesus' response to sinners wasn't to tell them that their sins were, "a gift from God," but rather to tell them, "Go and sin no more."

True biblical compassion demands that those who believe Christ's mission was indeed to redeem the lost must be willing to confront the lost with their sins. This can certainly be done in a loving manner. But for a Christian, condoning and encouraging the embrace of sin is far removed from anything remotely compassionate. Rather, it is the chilling fulfillment of Timothy's warning that,

> [T]he time will come when people will not put up with sound doctrine. Instead, to suit their own desires, they will gather around them a great number of teachers to say what their itching ears want to hear. They will turn their ears away from the truth and turn aside to myths.[4]

Exchanging the message of truth for the spirit of the age may be unbiblical, but many Christian leaders and ministers have found it is also conducive to building and maintaining large budgets. Lured by a love of money, they have become consumed with building facilities and providing entertainment more than offering rebuke and correction. As a result, the American church has never been this irrelevant in our history.

In light of these concerns, I know how easy it would be to give up. I know how easy it would be to give in.

In the quiet moments, surrounded by my family, I have even thought to myself how much more pleasant it would be to recede from the front lines and do as so many others do: go on about my daily life enjoying the fruits of liberty bestowed upon us by the patriots of our past. Just let someone else worry about future generations. After all, I have ball games to watch, a family to raise and church picnics to attend.

Yet, I know that if I yielded to that temptation of apathy, I would hear the relentless sounds of our proud past echoing in the chambers of my conscience. I would hear the drumbeats outside of Lexington. I would hear the voices from beyond the graves at the Gettysburg chapels. I would hear the pounding of the waves upon blood soaked beaches at Normandy. And they would be saying the same thing to me: Peter Heck, you are an American...act worthy of it.

And as I hold my little daughter's hand and brush the hair from her face, I realize how much I'm ready to act worthy of it. I realize how much those words "to secure the blessings of liberty to ourselves and our posterity" take on all new meaning. I realize anew why Scripture cautions us, "And let us not be weary in well doing: for in due season we shall reap, if we faint not."[5]

If there has ever been a time for us to be sons of Issachar, it is now. For such a time and such a place as this, we've been called. Grounded in truth, possessing an unquenchable thirst for answers to the questions that actually matter, and motivated by an eternal conviction that will not be exhausted or extinguished, we understand the times.

To the 78, we now know what we must do.

ENDNOTES

CHAPTER ONE
[1] http://religions.pewforum.org/reports

CHAPTER TWO
[1] Ferguson, Andrew. "Ride Along with Mitch," *The Weekly Standard*, June 5, 2010, Vol. 15, No. 37.
[2] *The Peter Heck Radio Show*, Archives
[3] Gore, Al. "Columbine Memorial Address," delivered April 25, 1999. Reprinted online:
http://www.americanrhetoric.com/speeches/algorecolumbine.htm
[4] Ibid.
[5] Cullen, Dave. "The Depressive and the Psychopath," *Slate*, April 20, 2004. Printed online: http://www.slate.com/id/2099203/
[6] Langman, Dr. Peter. "Columbine, Bullying, and the Mind of Eric Harris," Psychology Today, May 20, 2009. Printed online:
http://www.psychologytoday.com/blog/keeping-kids-safe/200905/columbine-bullying-and-the-mind-eric-harris
[7] The Holy Bible, Ezekiel 12:2 (New International Version)

CHAPTER THREE
[1] Stanley, Erik. "Yes: First Amendment Transcends Tax Code That Prohibits Free Speech," *Columbus Dispatch*, September 22, 2008. Reprinted online:
http://www.dispatch.com/live/content/editorials/stories/2008/09/22/Stanley22.ART_ART_09-22-08_A11_U0BCFJ7.html?sid=101
[2] *The Peter Heck Radio Show* archives.
[3] The Holy Bible, 1 Timothy 6:10 (New International Version)
[4] The Holy Bible, Luke 12: 49-53 (New International Version)
[5] Swindoll, Charles R. The Church Awakening: An Urgent Call for Renewal, NewYork: Faith Words, Hachette Book Group, 2010.
[6] Stern, Gary. "Televangelist Promises Hope, Positivity," *LoHud.com, powered by The Journal News*, April 22, 2009. Reprinted online:
http://www.lohud.com/article/2009904220354.
[7] Swindoll, Charles R. "It's Time to 'Restore the Years," Insight for Living Ministry, November 23, 2010. Audio available:
http://www.insightforliving.com/3/Archiveplayer.asp?id=1012244&date=11/23/2010
[8] http://religions.pewforum.org/reports
[9] The Holy Bible, 2 Corinthians 10:5 (New International Version)
[10] The Holy Bible, 1 Peter 3:15 (New International Version)
[11] Tocqueville, Alexis De. Democracy in America. New York: A.S. Barnes & Co., 1951, pg. 337.

[12] Ibid, pg. 332.

[13] Schaeffer, Francis A. The Great Evangelical Disaster, Wheaton, IL: Crossway Books, 1984, pg. 37.

CHAPTER FOUR

[1] The Holy Bible, Genesis 3:1 (New International Version)

[2] The Holy Bible, Genesis 3:2-3 (New International Version)

[3] The Holy Bible, Genesis 3:4 (New International Version)

[4] The Holy Bible, Genesis 3:5 (New International Version)

[5] Zengerle, Jason. "The Naked Guy," New York Times Magazine, December 31, 2006. Reprinted online: http://www.nytimes.com/2006/12/31/magazine/31naked.t.html.

[6] Time.com, Obama: People are Born Gay, Must Fight Back Against Cyberbullying, *Time Newsfeed*, 2010. reprinted online at: http://newsfeed.time.com/2010/10/15/obama-people-are-born-gay-must-fight-back-against-cyberbullying/.

[7] Graham, Michael, "'Pay grade' unartful dodge." Boston Herald, August 20, 2008. Reprinted online: http://www.bostonherald.com/news/opinion/op_ed/view.bg?articleid=1113869.

[8] *The Peter Heck Radio Show* archives.

[9] Ibid.

[10] Barna Research Group, Worldview Study, March 6, 2009. Reprinted online: http://www.barna.org/barna-update/article/21-transformation/252-barna-survey-examines-changes-in-worldview-among-christians-over-the-past-13-years.

CHAPTER FIVE

[1] The Holy Bible, Psalm 11:3 (New International Version)

[2] The Holy Bible, Acts 17:24a (New International Version)

[3] Hudson, Alex. "Why Haven't We Found Aliens Yet?" BBC News, December 14, 2010. Reprinted online: http://www.bbc.co.uk/news/science-environment-11982757.

[4] Ibid.

[5] Ibid.

[6] The Holy Bible, Genesis 1:1 (New International Version)

[7] The Holy Bible, Acts 17:24b (New International Version)

[8] The Holy Bible, Romans 7:15-19 (New International Version)

[9] *The Peter Heck Radio Show* archives.

[10] American Humanist Association press release November 23, 2009. Reprinted online: http://www.americanhumanist.org/news/details/2009-11-humanists-launch-first-ever-national-godless-holiday-.

[11] Jacoby, Jeff. "Created by God to be Good," *Boston Globe*, November 14, 2010. Reprinted online:

http://www.boston.com/bostonglobe/editorial_opinion/oped/articles/2
010/11/14/created_by_god_to_be_good/.

[12] Lewis, C.S. Mere Christianity, _____

[13] Martin, Glenn R. Prevailing Worldviews of Western Society Since
1500, Marion, IN: Triangle Publishing, 2006, pg. 37.

[14] The Holy Bible, Acts 17:24-25 (New International Version)

[15] The Holy Bible, Exodus 3:14 (New International Version)

[16] The Holy Bible, 1 Corinthians 13:12 (King James Version)

[17] D'Hippolito, Joseph. "Sympathy for a Devil," *FrontPageMagazine*,
November 20, 2006. Reprinted online:
http://archive.frontpagemag.com/readArticle.aspx?ARTID=1463.

[18] The Holy Bible, Acts 17:26 (New American Standard Version)

[19] The Holy Bible, Genesis 9:6 (New International Version)

[20] The Holy Bible, Acts 17:27 (New International Version)

[21] The Holy Bible, Matthew 5:13 (New International Version)

CHAPTER SIX

[1] Washington, George. *Farewell Address*, Newburyport, printed by
Angier March, 1800.

[2] Rasmussen, Scott. In Search of Self Government, Rasmussen Reports
LLC, Asbury Park, NJ: 2009.

[3] Jefferson, Thomas. *Declaration of Independence*, Philadelphia, PA:
July 4, 1776.

[4] Jefferson, Thomas. Letter to John Cartwright, Memorial Edition 16:44,
1824.

[5] Tocqueville, Alexis de. *Democracy in America* (2003), Penguin
Books, London, England, p. 596.

[6] Bastiat, Frederic. The Law, New York: Foundation for Economic
Education, 2007, pg. 69.

[7] Washington, George. *First Inaugural Address*, National Archives, April
30, 1789.

CHAPTER SEVEN

[1] Curry, Tom. GOP Candidate: 2010 Election is Like WWII,
MSNBC.com, May 5, 2010. Reprinted online:
http://www.msnbc.msn.com/id/36958211.

[2] Madison, James. *Speech in the Virginia Ratifying Convention on
Control of the Military*, June 16, 1788, in: *History of the Virginia Federal
Convention of 1788*, H.B. Grigsby ed. 1890, vol. 1, pg. 130.

[3] Ibid.

[4] Madison, James. *Federalist #51*, in: The Federalist, Philadelphia: J.B.
Kippincott & Co., 1864, pg. 397.

[5] Jefferson, Thomas. *First Inaugural Address*, National Archives, April
1801.

[6] Franklin, Benjamin. *Reply to the Governor*, Pennsylvania Assembly, November 11, 1755.

[7] Jefferson, Thomas. *Letter to Pierre Samuel Dupont de Nemours*, Memorial Edition 13:40, 1811.

[8] Politico. President Obama's Czars, September 8, 2009, printed online: http://www.politico.com/news/stories/0909/26779.html.

[9] Freire, J.P. "16,500 More IRS Agents Needed to Enforce Obamacare," Washington Examiner, March 18, 2010. Printed online: http://washingtonexaminer.com/blogs/beltway-confidential/16500-more-irs-agents-needed-enforce-obamacare.

[10] Varda, Francesca. "A Universal Court with Global Support," Coalition for the International Criminal Court, printed online: http://www.iccnow.org/?mod=usaicc.

[11] State of Arizona. Senate Bill 1070, reprinted online: http://www.azleg.gov/legtext/49leg/2r/bills/sb1070s.pdf.

[12] Archibold, Randal C. "Judge Blocks Arizona's Immigration Law," *New York Times*, July 29, 2010, pg A01. Reprinted online: http://www.nytimes.com/2010/07/29/us/29arizona.html.

[13] Seper, Jerry and Matthew Cella. "Signs in Arizona Warn of Smuggler Dangers," *The Washington Times*, August 31, 2010. Reprinted online: http://www.washingtontimes.com/news/2010/aug/31/signs-in-arizona-warn-of-smuggler-dangers/.

[14] Ibid.

[15] Davis, Susan. "Obama's Remarks on Service," Wall Street Journal, July 2, 2008. Reprinted online: http://blogs.wsj.com/washwire/2008/07/02/obamas-remarks-on-service/.

[16] Pelosi, Nancy. Floor Speech on Healthcare Vote, American Rhetoric, reproduced online: http://www.americanrhetoric.com/speeches/nancypelosihorhealthcarefinalvote.htm.

CHAPTER EIGHT

[1] Burke, Edmund. Reflections on the Revolution in France, 1790.

[2] Romney, Mitt. "Faith in America," delivered December 6, 2007 at the George H.W. Bush Presidential Library, College Station, TX. Reprinted online: http://www.nationalreview.com/articles/223036/faith-america/nro-primary-document.

[3] Hitchens, Christopher. "Holy Nonsense," in *Slate*: December 6, 2007. Reprinted online: http://www.slate.com/id/2179404/.

[4] Adams, John. October 11, 1798 in *The Works of John Adams, Second President of the United States*, Charles Francis Adams, ed., 1854, 9: 229.

[5] Ibid.

[6] Burke, Edmund. "Letter to a Member of the National Assembly," *Works*, 4:51-2, 1791.

[7] Rousseau, Jean-Jacques. As quoted in *A Dictionary of Thoughts: Being a Cyclopedia of Laconic Quotations from the Best Authors of the World, Both Ancient and Modern* (1908) by Tryon Edwards, p. 301.

[8] Duke, Selwyn. "Libertarianism's Folly: When 'Live and let Live' Fails," *American Thinker*, October 3, 2010. Published online: http://www.americanthinker.com/2010/10/libertarianisms_folly_when_liv.html.

[9] Golding, William. Lord of the Flies. London: Faber and Faber, 1954.

[10] Ibid.

[11] Ibid.

[12] Dostoevsky, Fyodor, translation by Garnett, Constance, revised by Matlaw, Ralph E. (1976, 1981). *The Brothers Karamazov*. New York: W.W. Norton.

[13] Nietzsche, Friedrich. *The Gay Science (1882): With a Prelude in Rhymes and an Appendix of Songs*. Translated, with commentary, by Walter Kaufmann. Vintage Books, March 1974.

[14] Seneca. *On Anger*, De Ira 1.15.

[15] Geiser, Dr. Norman, and Frank Turek. Legislating Morality. Minneapolis: Bethany House Publishers, 1998, pg. 60.

[16] Jefferson, Thomas. "A Summary View of the Rights of British America," 1774. Reprinted by University of Virginia Library Electronic Text Center Jefferson, Thomas, 1743-1826. A Summary View of the Rights of British America, p. 122, Electronic Text Center, University of Virginia Library. Reprinted online: http://etext.lib.virginia.edu/etcbin/toccer-new2?id=JefSumm.sgm&images=images/modeng&data=/texts/english/modeng/parsed&tag=public&part=all.

[17] Jefferson, Thomas. "Notes on the State of Virginia," 1781. Reprinted online: http://xroads.virginia.edu/~hyper/jefferson/intro.html.

[18] Keyes, Alan. Our Character, Our Future. Grand Rapids: Zondervan, 1996, pg. 12.

[19] Washington, George. *Farewell Address*, Newburyport, printed by Angier March, 1800.

[20] Baldwin, Abraham. Quoted by Chris Rushing in "Ten Truths About America's Christian Heritage," Coral Ridge Ministries, 2008. Printed online: http://www.coralridge.org/equip/10TruthsSeries/10%20Truths%20About%20Americas%20Christian%20Heritage/Forms/AllItems.aspx.

[21] Ibid.

[22] Ibid.

CHAPTER NINE

[1] Franklin, Benjamin. March 9, 1790, in a letter to Ezra Stiles, President of Yale University. Jared Sparks, editor, The Works of Benjamin Franklin (Boston: Tappan, Whittmore and Mason, 1838), Vol. X, p. 424.

[2] Madison, James. Memorial and Remonstrance Against Religious Assessments, in: *The Papers of James Madison*. Edited by William T. Hutchinson et al. Chicago and London: University of Chicago Press, 1962--77 (vols. 1--10); Charlottesville: University Press of Virginia, 1977--(vols. 11--).

[3] Adams, John. July 26, 1796, writing in his diary a disapproval of Thomas Paine's assertions. Norman Cousins, In God We Trust - The Religious Beliefs and Ideas of the American Founding Fathers (NY: Harper & Brothers, 1958), p. 99. L.H. Butterfield, ed., The Diary and Autobiography of John Adams (Cambridge, MA: The Belknap Press of Harvard University Press, 1962), Vol. 3, pp. 233-234. Edmund Fuller and David E. Green, God in the White House - The Faiths of American Presidents (NY: Crown Publishers, Inc., 1968), p. 25.

[4] Adams, John Quincy. July 4, 1821. John Wingate Thornton, The Pulpit of the American Revolution 1860 (reprinted NY: Burt Franklin, 1860; 1970), p. XXIX. Verna M. Hall, comp., Christian History of the Constitution of the United States of America (San Francisco: Foundation for American Christian Education, 1976), p. 372. Marshall Foster and Mary-Elaine Swanson, The American Covenant - The Untold Story (Roseburg, OR: Foundation for Christian Self-Government, 1981; Thousand Oaks, CA: The Mayflower Institute, 1983, 1992), p. 18.

[5] Adams, John Quincy. The Jubilee of the Constitution 13-14 (New York: Samuel Colman, 1839).

[6] Wilson, James. The Works of the Honorable James Wilson, Bird Wilson, editor (Philadelphia:
Lorenzo Press, 1804), Vol. I, pp. 104-106, "Of the General Principles of Law and Obligation."

[7] Hamilton, Alexander. The Papers of Alexander Hamilton 87 (Harold C. Syrett, ed., 1961) (February 23, 1775), quoting 1 William Blackstone, Commentaries on the Law of England 41 (Philadelphia: Robert Bell, 1771).

[8] Steiner, Bernard C. One Hundred and Ten Years of Bible Society Work in Maryland, 1810-1920 (Maryland Bible Society, 1921), p. 14.

[9] Rush, Benjamin. 1798. 1786, in "Thoughts upon the Mode of Education Proper in a Republic," published in Early American Imprints. Benjamin Rush, Essays, Literary, Moral and Philosophical (Philadelphia: Thomas and Samuel F. Bradford, 1798), p. 8, "Of the Mode of Education Proper in a Republic." The Annals of America, 20 vols. (Chicago, IL: Encyclopedia Britannica, 1968), Vol. 4, pp. 28-29.

[10] Ibid.

[11] Washington, George. May 7, 1789, in an address from the United States Senate. The Writings of George Washington, from the Original

Manuscript Sources 1749-1799, 39 vols. (Washington, D.C.: United States Government Printing Office, 1931-1944).

[12] Washington, George. October 28, 1789, in a letter to representatives of the ministers and elders of the Massachusetts and New Hampshire churches of the First Presbytery of the Eastward, Newburyport. The Massachusetts Centinel, December 5, 1789.

[13] Adams, John. March 23, 1798, in a Proclamation of a National Day of Humiliation, Fasting, and Prayer. James D. Richardson (U.S. Representative from Tennessee), ed., A Compilation of the Messages and Papers of the Presidents 1789-1897, 10 vols. (Washington, D.C.: U.S. Government Printing Office, published by Authority of Congress, 1897, 1899; Washington, D.C.: Bureau of National Literature and Art, 1789-1902, 11 vols., 1907, 1910), Vol. I, pp. 268-270.

[14] Paterson, William.

[15] Story, Justice Joseph.

[16] U.S. Constitution, Amendment I.

[17] Krannawitter, Thomas. "Establishment Clause is Misunderstood," reprinted online at: http://www.liberty-ca.org/articles/views/krannawitter2002_establishment.htm.

[18] Dwyer, Devin. "Christine O'Donnell: 'Separation of Church and State' in Constitution?" ABC News, October 19, 2010. Reprinted online (with video): http://abcnews.go.com/Politics/vote-2010-christine-odonnell-unclear-amendment-questions-separation/story?id=11916940.

[19] American Civil Liberties Union, "ACLU Responds to Appeals Court Ruling on Pledge of Allegiance," June 26, 2002. Reprinted online: http://www.aclu.org/religion-belief/aclu-responds-appeals-court-ruling-pledge-allegiance.

[20] United States Congress. January 19, 1853, Mr. Badger giving report of Congressional investigations in the Senate of the United States. The Reports of Committees of the Senate of the United States for the Second Session of the Thirty-Second Congress, 1852-53 (Washington: Robert Armstrong, 1853), pp. 1, 6, 8-9. Benjamin Franklin Morris, The Christian Life and Character of the Civil Institutions of the United States (Philadelphia: George W. Childs, 1864), pp. 324-327.

[21] United States Congress. August 1789, James Madison's response to Benjamin Huntington and Peter Sylvester regarding the First Amendment. Philip B. Kurland and Ralph Lerner, eds., The Founders' Constitution, 5 vols. (Chicago: University of Chicago Press, 1987), Vol. V, p. 93. M.E. Bradford, Religion & The Framers-The Biographical Evidence (Marlborough, NH: The Plymouth Rock Foundation, Inc., 1991), p. 12.

[22] United States Congress. January 19, 1853, Mr. Badger giving report of Congressional investigations in the Senate of the United States. The Reports of Committees of the Senate of the United States for the Second Session of the Thirty-Second Congress, 1852-53 (Washington: Robert

Armstrong, 1853), pp. 1, 6, 8-9. Benjamin Franklin Morris, The Christian Life and Character of the Civil Institutions of the United States (Philadelphia: George W. Childs, 1864), pp. 324-327.

[23] United States Congress. March 27, 1854, Mr. Meacham giving report of the House Committee on the Judiciary. Reports of Committees of the House of Representatives Made During the First Session of the Thirty-Third Congress (Washington: A.O.P. Nicholson, 1854), pp. 1, 6, 8-9. Benjamin Franklin Morris, The Christian Life and Character of the Civil Institutions of the United States (Philadelphia, PA: L. Johnson & Co., entered, according to Act of Congress, in the Clerk's Office of the District Court of the United States for the Eastern District of Pennsylvania, 1863; George W. Childs, 1864), pp. 317-324. "Our Christian Heritage," Letter from Plymouth Rock (Marlborough, NH: The Plymouth Rock Foundation), pp. 5-6.

[24] United States Congress. August 1789, Benjamin Huntington proposing adjustment to the wording of the First Amendment. M.E. Bradford, Religion & The Framers: The Biographical Evidence (Marlborough, NH: The Plymouth Rock Foundation, 1991), p. 11. Wells Bradley, "Religion and Government: The Early Days" (Tulsa, OK: Tulsa Christian Times, October 1992), p. 7.

[25] Lynch v. Donnelly, 465 U.S. 668 (1984).

[26] NEWDOW v. CONGRESS EGUSD SCUSD, No. 00-16423 December 04, 2002.

[27] Journals of the Continental Congress 1774-1789 (Washington, D.C.: Government Printing Office, 1905), book 146, Vol. VIII, pp. 731-735. Journal of the American Congress, 1774-1788 (Washington: 1823), Vol. II, pp. 261-262.

[28] Jared Sparks, ed., The Writings of George Washington 12 vols. (Boston: American Stationer's Company, 1837, NY: F. Andrew's, 1834-1847), Vol. XII, p. 119. James D. Richardson (U.S. Representative from Tennessee), ed., A Compilation of the Messages and Papers of the Presidents 1789-1897, 10 vols. (Washington, D.C.: U.S. Government Printing Office, published by Authority of Congress, 1897, 1899; Washington, D.C.: Bureau of National Literature and Art, 1789-1902, 11 vols., 1907, 1910), Vol. 1, p. 64.

[29] Geisler, Norman, and Frank Turek. Legislating Morality, Bethany House Publishers: 1998.

[30] *The Peter Heck Radio Show* archives.

CHAPTER TEN

[1] "Meet the Press," NBC News, August 17, 2008.

[2] Limbaugh, Rush. The Way Things Ought To Be, New York: Pocket Books, 1992, pg. 50.

[3] U.S. Supreme Court, Oral Arguments in *Roe v. Wade*, 410 U.S. 113 (1973). Reprinted online: http://www.oyez.org/cases/1970-1979/1971/1971_70_18/reargument.

[4] *Roe v. Wade*, 410 U.S. 113 (1973).

[5] Ibid.

[6] Tribe, Laurence. *Harvard Law Review*, 1973.

[7] Lazarus, Edward. *The Lingering Problems With Roe v. Wade*, 2002. Reprinted at www.FindLaw.com.

[8] Subcommittee on Separation of Powers to Senate Judiciary Committee S-158, Report, 97th Congress, 1st Session, 1981. Find more quotations and testimony at
http://www.abort73.com/index.php?/abortion/medical_testimony.

[9] Ibid.

[10] Ibid.

[11] PersonhoodUSA. "Video: Planned Parenthood Declares War on Science," Oct. 26, 2010, printed online:
http://www.personhoodusa.com/blog/video-planned-parenthood-declares-war-science. Full debate posted online:
http://eternityimpact.blogspot.com/2010/10/debate-video.html.

[12] Ibid.

[13] Ibid.

[14] Ibid.

[15] The Endowment for Human Development. "Prenatal Form and Function: 3 to 4 Weeks," posted online:
http://www.ehd.org/dev_article_unit4.php.

[16] *Planned Parenthood of Southeastern Pennsylvania v. Casey*, 505 U.S. 833 (1992).

[17] Bork, Robert. Slouching Towards Gomorrah: Modern Liberalism and American Decline (New York: Regan Books, HarperCollins, 1996, phk. ed), 111.

[18] Rosen, Jeffrey. "Worst Choice," in The New Republic, February 24, 2003. Reprinted online: http://www.tnr.com/article/worst-choice.

[19] Saddleback Civil Forum on the Presidency, August 17, 2008. Transcript reprinted online:
http://transcripts.cnn.com/TRANSCRIPTS/0808/17/se.01.html.

[20] Lincoln, Abraham. The "House Divided Against Itself" Speech. Quoted in The World's Famous Orations, America: II (1818-1865), 1906. Reprinted online: http://www.bartleby.com/268/9/22.html.

[21] *Bob Enyart Live* radio archives, aired December 2, 2008. Debate audio online: http://kgov.com/bel/20081202.

[22] Garrison, William Lloyd. "Defense of His Positions," 1854. Reprinted online:
http://teachingamericanhistory.org/library/index.asp?document=1432.

CHAPTER ELEVEN

[1] The Holy Bible, Mark 10:8 (New International Version)

[2] Gungor, Mark. Laugh Your Way to a Better Marriage: Unlocking the Secrets to Life, Love and Marriage, Simon and Schuster, 2008.

[3] The Holy Bible, Philippians 4:8 (New International Version).

[4] The Holy Bible, Romans 12:2 (New International Version).

[5] Quoted by Michael Crosby, Pornography: The Poison Pill, March 20, 2003. Reprinted online: www.believersweb.org/view.cfm?ID=209.

[6] Layden, Dr. Mary A. Testimony before the Senate Commerce Committee's Science, Technology,& Space Subcommittee, 2004.

[7] Ibid.

[8] Fatal Addiction: Dr. Dobson's Final Interview With Ted Bundy, *Focus on the Family*, January 23, 1989.

CHAPTER TWELVE

[1] Fitzpatrick, Brian. "Stunner! Kinsey Paid My Father to Rape Me," WorldNetDaily, October 17, 2010. Reprinted online: http://www.wnd.com/?pageId=213213.

[2] Ibid.

[3] Michael, Robert, Edward Laumann, John Gagnon, and Gina Bari Kolata. Sex in America: a Definitive Survey, Lebanon, IN: Hachette Book Group, 1995, pg. 172.

[4] Uniform Code of Military Justice, Article 134.

[5] Whitehurst, Lindsay. "Canadian Court Tackling Polygamy Question," Salt Lake Tribune, March 22, 2011. Reprinted online: http://www.sltrib.com/sltrib/news/51081832-78/polygamy-law-utah-court.html.csp.

[6] Ibid.

[7] Ibid.

[8] Ibid.

[9] DeGeneres, Ellen. Selected comments from *Ellen* (her syndicated TV show). Video clip can be viewed online at: http://www.youtube.com/watch?v=Od1Vh8lRvKY

[10] Gabbard, Mike. "Same Sex Fight Goes On," Island Voices, 1997. Reprinted online: http://www.e-z.net/wtv/oe050597.htm.

[11] The Holy Bible, John 8:11 (King James Version)

[12] Unruh, Bob. "Judges: People Have Only 'Qualified' Right to Christianity," WorldNetDaily, March 20, 2011. Reprinted online: http://www.wnd.com/index.php?fa=PAGE.printable&pageId=269573.

[13] TheIndyChannel.com, "Cookie Shop Accused of Refusing 'Coming Out Day' Order," October 1, 2010. Reprinted online: http://www.theindychannel.com/news/25231810/detail.html.

[14] The Washington Times, "Lesbian Wedding Lacks Photos," April 13, 2008. Reprinted online:

http://www.washingtontimes.com/news/2008/apr/13/lesbian-wedding-lacks-photos/.

[15] Bay City Television, Inc. "Lesbian Denied Fertility Treatment Settles Lawsuit," September 29, 2009. Reprinted online:
http://www.sandiego6.com/news/local/story/Lesbian-Denied-Infertility-Treatment-Settles/F7HIH7njS0a9PyEYC2lBNw.cspx.

[16] Colker, David. "EHarmony to Offer Same-Sex Matches After New Jersey Settlement," *Los Angeles Times*, November 19, 2008. Reprinted online:
http://latimesblogs.latimes.com/technology/2008/11/eharmony-goes-g.html.

[17] *Advocate*, 1985.

[18] *The Peter Heck Radio Show* archives.

[19] *Guide Magazine*, November 1987.

[20] Pope, Alexander. Essay on Man: Epistle 2. Reprinted online:
http://theotherpages.org/poems/pope-e2.html.

CHAPTER THIRTEEN

[1] The Holy Bible, Proverbs 22:6 (King James Version)

[2] Maslow, Abraham. "A Theory of Human Motivation," 1943. Reprinted online: http://www.abraham-maslow.com/m_motivation/Theory_of_Human_Motivation.asp.

[3] Rush, Benjamin. 1798. 1786, in "Thoughts upon the Mode of Education Proper in a Republic," published in Early American Imprints. Benjamin Rush, Essays, Literary, Moral and Philosophical (Philadelphia: Thomas and Samuel F. Bradford, 1798), p. 8, "Of the Mode of Education Proper in a Republic." The Annals of America, 20 vols. (Chicago, IL: Encyclopedia Britannica, 1968), Vol. 4, pp. 28-29.

[4] Ibid.

[5] Potter, Charles Francis (a signatory of the 1930 Humanist Manifesto I). Humanism: A New Religion (New York: Simon and Schuster, 1930), p. 128.

[6] Urey, Harold C. Quoted in Christian Science Monitor, January 4, 1962, p. 4.

[7] Kovacs, Joe. "Evangelists Claim Noah's Ark Found," *WorldNetDaily*, April 27, 2010. Printed online:
http://www.wnd.com/index.php?fa=PAGE.view&pageId=146369.

[8] Boyle, Alan. "Noah's Ark Found? Not So Fast," *MSNBC.com*, April 27, 2010. Printed online:
http://cosmiclog.msnbc.msn.com/_news/2010/04/27/4349742-noahs-ark-found-not-so-fast.

[9] Ibid.

[10] Ibid.

[11] Watts, Alex. "Scientists Unveil Missing Link in Evolution," Sky News, May 20, 2009. Printed online:

http://news.sky.com/skynews/Home/World-News/Missing-Link-
Scientists-In-New-York-Unveil-Fossil-Of-Lemur-Monkey-Hailed-As-
Mans-Earliest-Ancestor/Article/200905315284582.

[12] Handwerk, Brian. "Missing Link Found: New Fossil Links Human,
Lemurs?" National Geographic, May 19, 2009. Printed online:
http://news.nationalgeographic.com/news/2009/05/090519-missing-
link-found.html.

[13] Watts, Alex. "Scientists Unveil Missing Link in Evolution," Sky
News, May 20, 2009. Printed online:
http://news.sky.com/skynews/Home/World-News/Missing-Link-
Scientists-In-New-York-Unveil-Fossil-Of-Lemur-Monkey-Hailed-As-
Mans-Earliest-Ancestor/Article/200905315284582.

[14] Boyle, Alan. "Noah's Ark Found? Not So Fast," *MSNBC.com*, April
27, 2010. Printed online:
http://cosmiclog.msnbc.msn.com/_news/2010/04/27/4349742-noahs-
ark-found-not-so-fast.

[15] *Edwards v. Aguillard*, 482 U.S. 578 (1987).

[16] Sperry, Paul. "Teaching Johnny About Islam," Investor's Business
Daily, November 7, 2006. Reprinted online:
http://archive.frontpagemag.com/readArticle.aspx?ARTID=1711.

[17] Bozarth, G. Richard. "On Keeping God Alive," American Atheist (Nov
1977): 8; cited in John WhiteHead, Texas Tech Law Review (Winter
1978):40.

CHAPTER FOURTEEN

[1] Steinbeck, John. America and Americans, and selected nonfiction.
Penguin Books: New York, 2002, pg. 403

[2] Flynn, Dan. "Master of Deceit," *Front Page Magazine*, June 3, 2003.
Printed online:
http://archive.frontpagemag.com/readArticle.aspx?ARTID=17914#.

[3] Ibid.

[4] Handlin, Oscar. "Arawaks." *American Scholar* 49 (autumn 1980): 546-
50.

[5] Lincoln, Abraham. The Gettysburg Address, 1863.

[6] D'Souza, Dinesh. First Things.

[7] Ibid.

[8] D'Souza, Dinesh. What's So Great About America? Regnery
Publishing, Inc.: Washington, D.C., 2002, pp. 70-71.

[9] Gilbert, Kathleen. "NEA General Counsel Complains of Attacks from
'Right-Wing Bastards," *LifeSiteNews*, July 9, 2009. Printed online:
http://www.lifesitenews.com/news/archive/ldn/2009/jul/09070905.

[10] Ibid.

[11] Ibid.

[12] Carl, Michael. "NEA: Let's Celebrate Communism!" *WorldNetDaily*,
July 29, 2010. Printed online: http://www.wnd.com/?pageId=184721.

[13] National Education Association. "Recommended Reading: Saul Alinsky, The American Organizer." Printed online: http://www.nea.org/tools/17231.htm.

[14] Carl, Michael. "NEA: Let's Celebrate Communism!" *WorldNetDaily*, July 29, 2010. Printed online: http://www.wnd.com/?pageId=184721.

[15] NEA's Guide to the 'Extreme Right,' Overview and Introduction to the Extreme Right: A State's Approach," National Education Association, 1996.

[16] Dunphy, John. "A Religion for a New Age," The Humanist magazine, January-February 1983 [Volume 43, Number 1].

[17] The Holy Bible, Genesis 3:5 (King James Version)

CHAPTER FIFTEEN

[1] The Holy Bible, 1 Chronicles, 12:32 (New International Version)

[2] General references to Rev. Joe Wright's "Prayer for Repentance," delivered to the Kansas House of Representatives in January of 1996 and Bob Russell's prayer delivered at the 1995 Kentucky Governor's Prayer Breakfast.

[3] Gosier, Cicely. "Priest Says Being Gay a 'Gift' from God," CBNNews, January 25, 2009. Reprinted online: http://www.cbn.com/CBNnews/526476.aspx.

[4] The Holy Bible, 2 Timothy 4:3 (New International Version)

[5] The Holy Bible, Galatians 6:9 (King James Version)

SPECIAL ACKNOWLEDGEMENT

Chapter Fourteen's quote from Dinesh D'Souza comes from the book *What's So Great About America?* by Dinesh D'Souza. Copyright©2002. Published by Regnery Publishing, Inc. All rights reserved. Reprinted by special permission of Regnery Publishing Inc., Washington, D.C.

Made in the USA
Middletown, DE
03 February 2020